M000120313

A Mother's Work

A Mother's Work

How Feminism, the Market, and Policy Shape Family Life

NEIL GILBERT

Yale University Press New Haven and London

Published with assistance from the Louis Stern Memorial Fund.

Copyright © 2008 by Yale University.
All rights reserved.
This book may not be reproduced, in whole or in part, including illustrations, in any form (beyond that copying permitted by Sections 107 and 108 of the U.S. Copyright Law and except by reviewers for the public press), without written permission from the publishers.

Set in Minion type by Integrated Publishing Solutions, Grand Rapids, Michigan.
Printed in the United States of America by Thomson-Shore, Inc., Dexter, Michigan.

Library of Congress Cataloging-in-Publication Data
Gilbert, Neil.
A mother's work : how feminism, the market, and policy shape family life / Neil Gilbert.
p. cm.
Includes bibliographical references and index.
ISBN 978-0-300-11967-1 (cloth : alk. paper)
1. Working mothers—United States. 2. Work and family—United States. 3. Women in the professions—United States. 4. Family policy—United States. 5. Feminist theory—United States. I. Title.
HQ759.48.G55 2008
306.874'3—dc22 2007034309

A catalogue record for this book is available from the British Library.

The paper in this book meets the guidelines for permanence and durability of the Committee on Production Guidelines for Book Longevity of the Council on Library Resources.

10 9 8 7 6 5 4 3 2 1

To Bekki

Contents

Acknowledgments

In the course of writing this book, my thinking has benefited from ongoing conversations about motherhood and family policy with a stimulating community of scholars at the University of California, Berkeley. Coming from more than half a dozen disciplines, friends and colleagues at the Center for Child and Youth Policy and in the Berkeley Family Forum book club have collaborated on several edited volumes over the years and meet regularly to review books and share their research. For intellectual companionship that embraces spirited discussion of touchy subjects, I am indebted to Mary Ann Mason, Jill Duerr Berrick, Steve Sugarman, Carolyn Cowan, Phil Cowan, Ira Ellman, Paula Fass, Bruce Fuller, Alison Gopnik, Norton Grubb, Sylvia Gundelman, Stephen Hinshaw, Joan Hollinger, David Kirp, Jane Mauldon, Dan Perlstein, Richard Scheffler, Ruth Rosen, Karen Sokal-Gutierrez, Susan Stone, Joan Williams, Gillian Lester, Melissa Murray, Catherine Albiston, Margaret Weir, and Ruth Zafran. Although I have benefited from their wisdom and good counsel, it is hard to imagine, if experience is any guide, that these fine people would not take issue with some of the analyses and conclusions drawn in this book—the Berkeley Family Forum has never to my recollection discussed a volume about which its members failed to detect many areas for improvement. Since we often learn most from engaging those with whom we differ, I take comfort in contributing to the process.

While working on this book, I also had the good fortune of being able to submit my nascent ideas to public scrutiny on various occasions. In 2004, preliminary formulations for several sections of the book were presented at a conference sponsored by the Institute on Culture, Religion and World Affairs at Boston University, and later appeared in *Society* ("Family Life: Sold on Work," *Society* 42:3 [March/April 2005], 12–17) and *The Public Interest* ("What Do Women Really Want?" *The Public Interest* 158 [Winter 2005], 21–38). I am grateful to the conference organizers Peter Berger and Jonathan Imber for providing a venue to exchange views with an exciting group of social thinkers including Judith Kleinfeld, Angela Dillard, Karlyn Bowman, Rita Simon, Claudia Winkler, Andrew Kleinfeld, and Brigitte Berger. I had a chance to partake in a wide-ranging discussion about family policy during the 2005 meeting A Dialogue for a New Moral Agenda, organized by Amitai Etzioni at the Institute for Communitarian Policy Studies at George Washington University. In 2006, a public lecture on work and family life, sponsored by the Institute for Human Sciences in Vienna, was followed by an engaging conversation with the European audience, which ended only when we were informed that the food at the reception was getting cold. And in 2007 I gave the Sydney Ball lecture at Oxford University, which drew on several lines of analysis in my manuscript; this event was capped by a spirited evening of collegial debate during a memorable dinner hosted by George Smith. I wish to thank the sponsors of these learned gatherings for the kind receptions afforded to me, and the many participants for the benefits of their constructive feedback. Although my work has profited from these occasions to test initial analyses in public fora, needless to say none of the people or institutions mentioned bear responsibility for any deficiencies that remain in the final results.

I am obliged to my doctoral student Jing Guo for assistance in collecting and organizing data and to Lorretta Morales for handling many of the local chores of manuscript preparation. I was pleased and astonished by the intellectual force with which Keith Condon of Yale University Press gently wielded his red pencil. His incisive comments were always on the mark. I am also indebted to my production editor Jessie Hunnicutt for conducting a remarkably thorough and constructive review of the manuscript. I wish to express my appreciation to the family members who established the Milton and Gertrude Chernin Chair in Social Services and Social Welfare at the University of California, Berkeley, which provided generous support for my research on this book.

Special gratitude is owed to my children, Evan, Jesse, Nathaniel, and Nicole, for the wonder and joy they impart on the existential roller coaster of family life. Finally, my deepest appreciation goes to my wife, Bekki, whose care and guidance have kept the ride on track. A lawyer, a gifted scholar of social policy, and an inspirational mother, she has lent warm encouragement to my work along with valuable insights on motherhood, feminism, and the difference between independence and self-sufficiency.

Introduction

"What do you think family life will look like in fifty years?" was a question I posed to the Berkeley Family Forum, a book club of academics whose leisure time was spent doing what they were normally paid to do on the job. That evening we were dissecting Stephanie Coontz's provocative work on the history of marriage, which concluded that married life today has become more fulfilling yet more fragile than in the past.[1] As to the future, she believed that marriage was unlikely to be revived as the primary source of commitment and caregiving in modern society. Historians are of course much better at recounting the past than forecasting what is to come. Among the historians, lawyers, and social scientists in the book club, nobody ventured to predict the normative contours of family life fifty years from now.

If the question had been asked in the same living room fifty years earlier, however, I think we would have felt more confident trying to envision where family life was headed. In the mid-1950s many of us might have predicted that the contours of family life would remain fairly stable, looking today much as they did then—and we would have been dead wrong. Who would have guessed the remarkable changes waiting just around the corner? Soon after the 1950s, family size declined, divorce rates doubled, the labor-force participation rate of married women with children under eighteen years of age tripled, unimaginable levels of domestic violence and child abuse came to light, single parenthood soared, and cohabitation outside of marriage mounted. College life changed from sex-segregated dorms to coed housing with unisex bathrooms. In 1972 the Massachusetts Superior Court convicted William Baird of the illegal act of giving a contraceptive device to a college student during a lecture on contraception at Boston University. The decision was sustained by the State Supreme Judicial Court.[2] Nowadays contraceptive devices are frequently distributed to students in public high schools.

These changes in social relations and sexual mores have yielded both costs and benefits. Whether things are ultimately better or worse is open to interpretation—and depends on what they are compared to.[3] In retrospect, the 1950s were an unusually stable period for the American family, often characterized as a unique interlude in an otherwise long tradition of change and anxiety about the fragility of family life.[4] Be that as it may, the 1950s remain a common reference point against which family life is compared today, much more so than the era of the Great Depression, the Roaring Twenties, Victorian England, or the Holy Roman Empire. People who lament that family life as we once knew it is going to hell in a handbasket are thinking about the lost stability of the 1950s, but they are overlooking the lack of employment opportunities and other constraints on lifestyle options for women of that period. Today women have more control over the course and rhythm of their lives than ever before. They also struggle with more choices about how to achieve self-fulfillment. One of the most challenging decisions concerns how much of their labor to invest in the work of motherhood and how much in paid employment. This book is about that choice.

An introduction customarily offers the lay of the land, stakes the contextual boundaries, and gives readers an idea of where the chapters are headed, why the journey was undertaken, and what it signifies. In this instance the title—*A Mother's Work: How Feminism, the Market, and Policy Shape Family Life*—pretty much tells the story. This book explores the modern-day struggle to combine employment and family life. Examining recent trends and policies, I seek to explain the social dynamics that influence this struggle and to clarify whose interests are truly being served.

Part I frames the social context by looking at how women have responded to the tensions and opportunities created by the contraceptive revolution, civil rights advances, and the changing structure of the labor market since the 1960s. Recent claims submit that after a tidal wave of increased labor-force participation, women are now "opting out" of the workforce and returning home to give birth and raise children. I appraise these claims in light of evidence that suggests that while some movement is under way, it is still too early to tell whether a sea change is in the making. Although the future remains uncertain, evidence from the past forty years illustrates a compelling long-term trend. By all accounts, there has been a significant decline in the pursuit of motherhood as usually identified by childbearing, childrearing, and household production. The rate of childlessness has climbed to historic proportions for a period of relative peace and prosperity. Those women who do have children are producing smaller families and are increasingly farming out the early years of intensive child care to other people, as mothers shift their labor from the household to the marketplace.

What explains these changes? Some might say that women, having finally been given the chance, are now simply doing what they want—and leave it at that. Others might argue that economic necessity is driving mothers into the market. I offer a different view, which suggests that more than need and personal inclination are at work. My main line of analysis, which informs Part II, is based on three assertions: that the culture of capitalism undervalues the economic worth of childrearing activities and domestic production, that prevailing feminist expectations overestimate the social and emotional benefits of labor-force participation, and that the family-friendly policies of the welfare state create incentives that reinforce the norms and values of capitalism and feminism. As a result, since the 1960s women's choices about how much of their lives to invest in childrearing and paid employment have been made in a social context that is heavily stacked against motherhood—regardless of women's individual needs and predilections.

There are a lot of questions to consider when delving into this topic: Does having children make economic sense? Is the sexual division of labor a rational choice? How has the time devoted to child care by employed and nonemployed mothers changed in recent decades? What are the different agendas associated with preschool child care? How are the outcomes of preschool child care measured—and who ultimately benefits from these services? To what extent is the powerful arsenal of so-called family-friendly policies in European countries truly friendly to family life?

Of course, the argument that the labor of motherhood is undervalued, and that the personal benefits of paid work are overestimated, is not true for all women. Clearly, some women's interests are well served by the social forces emanating from the culture of capitalism, feminist expectations about work, and family-policy incentives that support an early start and continuous participation in the labor market. Indeed, these influences endorse and advance the interests of women with the aptitude and ambition to succeed in high-status, stimulating, and well-rewarded careers—those of the occupational elite. But only a small proportion of working men and women ever make it into this upper echelon of professional and corporate life. The rest tend to retire from the labor force as soon as they can. Politicians, academics, think-tank analysts, journalists, and most others who think, talk, and write about how to balance work and family life tend to labor in the groves of the occupational elite, which is one reason why much of the policy discourse in this realm emphasizes the financial, emotional, and social benefits of paid work—benefits enjoyed by this class.

The standard family-policy discourse emphasizes how best to harmonize paid work and domestic life through initiatives that facilitate a seamless transition from school to the paid labor force and encourage staying the course of paid employment with as little interruption as possible. This approach follows the model typically adhered to by men under the traditional division of labor in family life—that is, making an early start and maintaining a continuous record of employment. To achieve equality in the labor market, women have to start as quickly and remain active as long as men. Although this male model is well suited for women aiming toward the pinnacles of professional and corporate life, it may be less attuned to the needs and interests of working- and middle-class mothers in average jobs that are neither very high paying nor emotionally all that gratifying.

The conventional ledger on family policy calls for public investment in such measures as high-quality nonmaternal child care, parental leave incentives that encourage fathers to assume a greater share of child-care responsibility, and flexible working hours—all of which are designed to assist mothers in maintaining paid employment while raising young children. Efforts to reconcile work and family through policies that promote concurrent labor-force participation and childrearing are important, serve the interests of many women, and undoubtedly deserve public support. However, this model offers few, if any, benefits that endorse and advance the interests of mothers who might prefer to take a sequential approach to work and family life—investing their labor entirely in childrearing activities during the preschool years and then moving into employment as their children become more independent and spend most of the day in school. Thus, my analysis concludes by comparing the sequential and concurrent approaches and presenting some thoughts on how to balance family-friendly policies with more choices and a greater public appreciation for a mother's work.

I
Responding to the Tensions of Work and Family

Chapter I
The Social Context: Motherhood in Decline?

Not too long ago, caring for children was unquestionably the most important activity that women performed in society. Before the 1960s, it was customary for mothers not to work outside the home, a convention acknowledged and reinforced by social policy. For example, Aid to Dependent Children (ADC), a program under the Social Security Act of 1935, gave cash grants to single mothers so they could stay home and care for their children.[1] But during the 1960s, normative views and policies concerning the role of motherhood began to shift in response to feminist demands for social and economic equality—and, some might add, in response to labor-force needs. The changing expectations surrounding motherhood are evident in the transformation of ADC, which by 1996 had morphed into Temporary Assistance for Needy Families (TANF), a program that aimed to move women with young children into the labor force.[2] By the late 1990s, women were having fewer children, and mothers were increasingly delegating child-care responsibilities to others as they entered the paid workforce in what were historic proportions for peaceful times.

Since the dawn of the twenty-first century, however, word has been spreading that a revival of home care is under way, with women returning in droves to domestic life, leaving lucrative careers to give birth and raise their children. Reports of this trend have received considerable media attention. Under the front-page headline "Putting Family First," the April 2002 issue of *People* magazine told of such celebrities as Sissy Spacek, Demi Moore, and Jodie Foster finding more joy and meaning in being mothers than movie stars. Three months later *Vogue* ran a glossy thirteen-page spread about supermodels taking time out for motherhood.

The fluffy stories in *People* and *Vogue* were not so much hard news as rumors of a trend. Since these magazines rank low as providers of news and opinion in feminist intellectual circles, the stories of childbearing and home care among the rich and famous did not create much of a stir. But around the same time, Sylvia Ann Hewlett's book *Creating a Life: Professional Women and the Quest for Children* surfaced, provoking the feminist community. Hewlett found that 42 percent of the high-achieving women in her study were childless after age forty (a figure that climbed to 49 percent among the women in her sample who earned $100,000 or more) and that many women who did have children had only one.[3]

Hewlett was charged with delivering a dangerous antifeminist message. If taken seriously, Garance Franke-Ruta maintained, her findings might lead to more young women having children, "but so too will more of them get divorced, become single moms, or opt not to become high achievers in the first place."[4] Citing data from a much larger survey than Hewlett's sample of 520, Franke-Ruta offered a more optimistic picture of the marriage and childbearing prospects for high-achieving women. She also reported on a *Fortune* magazine study of female CEOs, presidents, and managing directors of major corporations, which found that 29 percent of the most powerful women in business were childless.[5] (Although this figure is about 40 percent lower than that of the $100,000-plus earners in Hewlett's sample, it is also about 50 percent higher than the national rate of childlessness among women in 2002.)

For most men and women it requires many years of education and hard work to scale the upper peaks of the corporate world or to gain entry to the most prestigious chambers of professional life. Hewlett's controversial message that the long struggle for career success is not conducive to childbearing was reinforced by a 2002 cover story in *Time* magazine, which publicized how much the odds against fertility increased with age. Citing findings from the Centers for Disease Control and Prevention, the authors reported that by the age of forty-two women had only a 7.8 percent chance of having a baby with their own eggs, because at that age 90 percent of the eggs were abnormal.[6] (Mother Nature, I might note, has not exempted men's reproductive capacities from the ravages of Father Time—as men age, their sperm count declines and the likelihood of chromosome abnormality increases.)

An "Opt-Out Revolution"?

In 2003 the various rumors and claims about the challenges of managing work and family life crystallized into news of a full-scale retreat to hearth and home. Detecting the start of an "opt-out revolution," Lisa Belkin's *New York Times Magazine* article told of accomplished professional women leaving high-powered jobs to stay home with their children.[7] She predicted the coming of a new era—and raised quite a commotion among feminists, who criticized Belkin for, among other things, focusing on only a small segment of elite professionals who had married other elite professionals and could afford to stay home.[8] A piece in the *Boston Globe* portrayed these mothers as the status symbol of a new privileged class.[9] Several months later, in March 2004, the cover of *Time* showed a young child clinging to its mother's leg alongside the headline, "The Case for Staying Home: Why More Young Moms Are Opting Out of the Rat Race."[10]

Two years after Belkin's initial report, talk of the "revolution" was still going strong. On January 1, 2006, the op-ed page of the *New York Times* featured David Brooks looking back over the essays of the previous year and finding "an amazing number that dealt with domesticity. That's because the deeper you get into economic or social problems—national competitiveness, poverty, school performance, incarceration—the more you realize the answers lie with good parenting and good homes."[11] And in March 2007, Joan Williams's analysis of 119 news stories about women leaving the workforce found that three-fourths of these articles called attention to the emotional pulls drawing mothers back into domestic life while ignoring the pushes of workplace discrimination, inflexibility, and lack of adequate child care.[12]

The media emphasis on the new life awaiting mothers at home coincided with the birth of "maternal feminism," part of a movement spearheaded by the Motherhood Project at the Institute for American Values.[13] Calling for greater involvement of mothers in their children's lives, the project's director, Enola Aird, stated that "too many parents are not sufficiently attentive to the project of forming the character and morality of their children, losing touch with the spirit of 'home training.'"[14] Maternal feminism has not elicited universal enthusiasm. Expressing the concerns of earlier advocates of feminism,

Maureen Dowd voiced dismay at the dire consequences awaiting stay-at-home mothers. "If we flash forward to 2030," she asked, "will we see all those young women who thought trying to Have It All was a pointless slog, now middle-aged and stranded in suburbia, popping Ativan, struggling with rebellious teenagers, deserted by husbands for younger babes, unable to get back into a work force they never tried to be part of?"[15]

Although news of a social upheaval is in the air, on the ground it is hard to say exactly what is happening. Despite the flood of essays celebrating or complaining about the resurgence of motherhood and domestic life, evidence that we are in the midst of an opt-out revolution is not entirely persuasive. Both the *New York Times Magazine* and *Time* stories are based mainly on evocative anecdotes. One of Belkin's subjects, a Princeton graduate, observes, "I think some of us are swinging to a place we enjoy, and can admit we enjoy, the stereotypical role of female/mother/caregiver. . . . I think we were born with these feelings."[16] Women with law degrees from Princeton and MBAs from Harvard musing about the allure of staying home to change diapers may be an absorbing human-interest story, but in this case the plural of anecdote is not data.

Accounts of the opt-out revolution do cite some hard facts, however. For example, 22 percent of mothers with graduate degrees are at home with their children, 33 percent of women with MBAs do not work full time, and 26 percent of women approaching the most senior levels of management do not want to be promoted. Yet, cross-sectional data that provide a snapshot of facts at one point in time do not tell us whether there is a revolution afoot or the direction in which it might be headed. With information of this sort one needs a Ouija board to detect a social trend. To what extent has the proportion of mothers with college or graduate degrees who stay home with their children varied since 1970? Belkin notes that 57 percent of mothers from the Stanford University class of 1981 stayed home with their young children for at least a year in the first decade after graduation. There is no indication, however, whether that high percentage of at-home mothers has increased, decreased, or remained the same over time. And even if there has been an increase since 1970 in the percentage of women who stay home after obtaining college or graduate degrees from elite universities, one must bear in mind that the proportion of women with college or graduate degrees was significantly lower in 1970 than today.

Data on the work histories of more than ten thousand women in the 1976 entering class of thirty-four elite colleges and universities revealed that more than fifteen years after graduation almost 60 percent had never been out of work for more than six months at a time for reasons other than education. At the same time about 33 percent of the women graduates with children had out-of-work spells of more than two years, and 18 percent had out-of-work spells of more than five years. By comparison, only 3 percent of the male graduates had out-of-work spells of more than two years.[17]

These data can be read several ways. One could interpret the numbers to show that a healthy majority of women who graduated from elite institutions twenty-five years ago stayed the course with a continuous record of paid employment in their chosen careers. And one could go on to say that a substantial proportion of mothers who graduated from elite institutions during this period took a break from paid work for more than two years, and that many were unemployed for more than five years. At the very least, these figures suggest that at any time since 1980 a resourceful journalist could have found a sample of female graduates from elite colleges and universities who left work for some period to stay at home and raise their children. Indeed, such stories surfaced from time to time. But the question of whether the previous pattern of taking time out from paid employment has increased dramatically among women who graduated after 2000, as well as among those who never went to college, remains difficult to answer. Is an opt-out revolution upon us? On this matter I would concur with Claudia Goldin's 2006 assessment that "the jury must remain out for at least another decade."[18]

Having said that, however, there are some indications that although the winds of change may not have swept through the market, a slight breeze is in the air, and it may be gathering momentum. This inkling of change involves the leveling off of female labor-force participation in 1998, which turned into a slight decline of 0.8 percent between 2000 and 2004. Looking more closely we find that women ages twenty-five to fifty-four accounted for 69 percent of the female labor force in 2004. Among this age group, the decline in labor-force participation from 2000 to 2004 was two percentage points—much of it ascribed to the changing behavior of college-educated, married women with children under the age of three.[19] Although this decline hardly qualifies as a headline-grabbing social revolution, such a drop over a four-year period is not trivial. If this rate of decline were to continue, within virtually one generation the percentage of women in the labor force would have fallen nearly to the level of the mid-1960s. That would indeed qualify as revolutionary.

Of course, the recent decline might be just a temporary blip or a signal that participation is leveling off—after all, the rate could not rise forever. Or it could be a harbinger of a readjustment in career patterns, one which introduces a season for childrearing into the course of work and family life. Rather than opting out of the labor force completely, those who have left work in recent years may be taking time out for motherhood and planning to reenter the workplace sometime down the line. Perhaps they are extending the length of time out that was taken by many of the women with children who graduated from elite colleges and universities in the early 1980s. The recent pattern of movement into the labor force shows that while the overall rate decreased between 2000 and 2004 for the large group of women between ages twenty-five and fifty-four, there was a 4 percent increase in participation among the smaller cohort of women over fifty-four years of age.

Within these broad categories of age, however, something else is going on. A more compelling trend is evident when we narrow our focus to the behavior of college-educated, married women with young children. In this group we find that the labor-force participation rate declined by about 8 percent between 1994 and 2004. (The 8 percent fall excludes working mothers on maternity leave under the Family and Medical Leave Act, who are officially counted as employed.) This recent decline contrasts sharply with the experience of the 1980s, during which an increasing proportion of married women with young children joined the paid labor market.[20] The shift in behavior among college-educated mothers not only deviates from the pattern of the previous decade but seems somewhat at odds with the rational calculation of economic gain, which encourages women to capitalize on their educational investment by going to work.

What accounts for this behavioral change among highly educated young women, who consciously invested in years of education, largely to increase their human capital in preparation for well-paid employment? Some might say that these women could well afford to leave work because they were more likely to have high-earning husbands than women without advanced educations. But this was also true in the 1980s, when labor-force participation among women with the same family and educational characteristics increased markedly. Another possible explanation for the decline from 1994 to 2004 could be that changes in wages, market opportunities, or family income reduced the women's commitment to the labor market. For example, college-educated mothers might have been dissuaded from working if their weekly earnings declined after 1994 or if their husband's earnings increased at a higher rate than in the 1980s. But neither of these changes occurred.[21] Nor was there an increase in overt discrimination or other barriers that might have inhibited labor-force participation. After examining the evidence on a range of alternative explanations, Katherine Bradbury and Jane Katz found that the decline in paid employment might reflect changing social norms, particularly during an era when traditional gender roles are in flux.[22]

A fraction of the drop in women entering the labor market could be attributed to slightly higher unemployment in 2004. In another study, Julie Hotchkiss carefully estimated the impact of changes in unemployment rates along with other measurable characteristics such as educational attainment, marriage, childbearing, race, and income. She concluded that these factors, which economists usually rely upon, do not fully explain the declining labor-force participation of women between 2000 and 2004.[23] As with Bradbury and Katz, her explanation falls to more ethereal social properties—"unobservable" norms and values—which are harder to document and quantify than demographic traits. Despite this intangible quality, norms and values have a very real influence on human affairs, which becomes most evident in periods of change.

Changes in social norms involve shifts in shared expectations about acceptable and desirable behavior. These expectations are learned, usually through socialization in childhood;

they may change over time—often slowly—but how this change comes about is not entirely understood. Norms governing family life in the 1930s, for example, prescribed that wives stay at home to care for children and elderly relatives. This widespread expectation regarding the role of motherhood was endorsed by the 1935 Social Security legislation, not only through the formation of ADC but also through the provision of a dependents' benefit. Under this benefit, nonworking spouses qualified for a pension payment equal to 50 percent of the primary benefit earned by the retired wage earner. But the expectations of motherhood changed as women entered the labor force en masse. Today the dependents' benefit is a source of considerable inequity. After paying social security taxes, many working wives end up qualifying for the same pension as the dependents' benefit received by stay-at-home mothers—and sometimes their pensions are even lower than the dependents' benefit of stay-at-home mothers.[24]

Changes in social values involve a modification of the shared beliefs that people hold dear to their conceptions of well-being and the good life—that is, the level of importance attributed to material wealth, status, emotional satisfaction, family duty, professional achievement, social relationships, liberty, education, and individual happiness. Anthony Trollope's "The Lady of Launay" conveys the world of upper-class Victorian values, wherein the import of family duty prevails over individual happiness. In the story, the Lady ponders what to do about the untoward romance between her ward, Bessy, and her son, Philip: "Of course she wanted them all to be happy. But happiness was to her thinking of much less importance than her duty; and at the present moment her duty and Bessy's duty and Philip's duty were so momentous that no idea of happiness ought to be considered in the matter."[25] The duty to which the Lady refers is her obligation to advance the wealth and social position of the house of Launay by arranging a more advantageous marriage for her son. Today, although duty to family is still believed to be a good thing, modern divorce rates suggest that it is no longer as fervently valued as in the Lady of Launay's time. As with normative expectations about proper behavior, social beliefs about what is good and important in life are learned, mostly in childhood. Some social values are extremely durable; others change over time—and the dynamics of change are ambiguous.

Efforts to explain the recent decline in women's labor-force participation as a response to changing opportunities and incentives such as rising unemployment rates, increases in nonwage income (for example, spouse's income or investment earnings), declining wages, and rising levels of educational achievement present a logical set of material reasons for how people decide to lead their lives. These reasons are more agreeable to policy makers than explanations that point to changing norms and values. It is easier to design policies that might affect, for example, wages and education. By contrast, norms and values, while not immune to policy incentives, are less predictable, and therefore less easy to control. Indeed, changes in norms and values sometimes seem to come out of the air, particularly in regard to expected behavior in relations between men and women. For example, as a young man growing up in the 1950s, I was taught that on entering a building or store it was proper to hold the door open for women. By the late 1960s that gentle behavior was as likely as not to ignite the ire of many women, who were marching to a different beat than their mothers. Today, holding the door open appears to have become more acceptable, or at least less of a faux pas.[26] Similarly, in the 1950s men were expected to foot the tab for dinner.

By the 1960s women were demanding to pay their share of the bill. Today, women continue to reach for their purse, but if a man readily accepts a woman's offer to pay, that's probably their last dinner together!

Prior to the 1970s it was customary for a woman to assume her husband's surname upon marriage. Between the 1970s and 1990 there was a significant deviation from this custom as increasing proportions of women, particularly college graduates, retained their surnames upon marriage. During this period the age at which women first married increased, as did their years of education and participation in the labor force—and so did divorce rates. By marrying later and investing more time in education and careers, women accumulated social capital under their maiden names, which they might have been reluctant to forfeit—particularly with the probability of marriage ending in divorce rising to around 50 percent by 1990. Since the 1990s, however, the trend toward keeping one's family name appears to have reversed. Data based on Massachusetts birth records suggest that the fraction of female college graduates who retained their surnames declined from 23 percent in 1990 to 17 percent in 2000. A similarly sharp reduction was found between women graduates in the Harvard class of 1980 who were married by 1990 and those in the class of 1990 who were married by 2000.[27] The faint drift toward more traditional customs might be seen as part of an emerging normative revision, which includes the leveling off and slight decline in labor-force participation among women.

Attributing the decline in labor-force participation to changing norms and values puts the issue in a realm of social life that is less exact than wages and levels of education. Life's exactitude is obvious, as G. K. Chesterton observed, "but its inexactitude is hidden; its wildness lies in wait." Although normative shifts tend to be clearly recognized after the fact, they are notoriously difficult to pinpoint in the early stages. At this juncture it is not yet clear whether the changes registered between 1994 and 2004 reflect a substantial shift in the timing of women's breaks from paid employment or a significant decrease in women's cumulative lifetime participation in the labor market. For Bradbury and Katz, the conspicuous fall in the participation rate of highly educated mothers remains a puzzling development.[28] And how this development might apply to broader adjustments in motherhood and family life in the late 1990s is also uncertain. Reviewing some of the short-term changes, Barbara Whitehead and David Popenoe find the best that can be said is that many of the trends "toward a weakening of family structure in the past few decades have slowed dramatically, and in some cases leveled off."[29]

Will the rate of women's labor-force participation begin to climb again after cooling off for a few years? Flatten out at a new level of equilibrium? Continue to decline? Develop an alternative pattern of distribution among different age groups? Or be reshaped by an explosion of part-time work and telecommuting? And how will this affect motherhood and family life? The next generation will tell what wildness lies in wait.

In the Meantime: The Other Revolution

The past may hold some keys to the future, but in 1960 there was little inkling that within one generation the majority of women with children would be actively engaged in the labor force—Betty Friedan's *Feminine Mystique* had yet to appear. There was even less of a clue that the U.S. fertility rate would decline by more than one-third, from 3.4 to 2.02 (just below the replacement rate of 2.1). Indeed, the oft-expressed public concern was that the United States would be swamped by overpopulation, a fear fanned by Paul Ehrlich's 1968 best-seller *The Population Bomb,* which predicted that major food shortages would lead to the starvation of 65 million Americans by 1989.[30]

At the moment, predictions of an opt-out revolution in the next generation lean on thin data and truncated trend lines. Despite the drop in labor-force participation among women with young children between 2000 and 2004, Heather Boushey contends that when the time frame is extended we find that mothers with high school or college degrees in 2004 were less likely to leave the labor market because of their children than those in 1984.[31] Indeed, viewed in a broader context, the changing patterns of employment reveal a more compelling story, one that involves long-term trends of a steady increase in women's labor-force participation alongside an equally steady decline in the percentage of men in the labor force.

Not only has the percentage of women joining the labor force climbed since the previous generation, but they are entering with more powerful credentials. Compared with the 1970s, a substantially larger percentage of women today are attending graduate school and earning high-status professional degrees. Between 1970 and 2002 the proportion of medical degrees awarded to women increased by almost 529 percent; law, 888 percent; business, more than 1,000 percent; and dentistry, 4,277 percent.[32] These are impressive advances, even when we consider that relatively modest numerical gains yield sizable changes in percentage points when starting from a low base. If one-third of all women receiving advanced degrees today were to opt out of their professions, the remaining two-thirds would still represent a noteworthy increase in women's employment in these areas over the past three decades.

As women have entered the labor force with more educational preparation, they have increasingly expressed a bent for entrepreneurial activity. Between 1997 and 2004 the number of companies owned by women climbed by 20 percent, or twice the 10 percent growth rate in the total number of U.S. businesses. Similar to most businesses, the vast majority of women-owned businesses were single-person enterprises.[33] Women's earnings have also risen in recent years. In 33 percent of the families with working wives, women earned more than their husbands in 2004—up from 24 percent in 1987.[34]

From a longitudinal perspective, the women currently opting out of jobs and professional careers to stay home with their children are at the margins of a profound lifestyle trend that has extended over the past several decades—a development deftly portrayed, some might say celebrated, in the media. After a six year run, the popular HBO series *Sex and the City* ended in 2004 with what was widely reported as a happy ending. Each of the four heroines, in their late thirties and early forties, had found love and commitment while pursuing gratifying careers. The series finale was a paean to love and individual fulfillment. But as for family life, these four vibrant, successful women approaching the terminus of their childbearing years ended up with only two marriages and one child between them. As a mirror of society, the media shift from kids bouncing off the walls in *The Brady Bunch* to the 0.25 fertility rate in *Sex and the City* several decades later clearly reflects the cultural and demographic trends during this period. *Sex and the City* was followed by *Desperate Housewives,* a popular network series whose title signifies its social commentary on the dark lives of stay-at-home mothers on Wisteria Lane.

In 2002, almost one in five women in their early forties were childless, close to double the proportion of childless women in 1976. Also during that quarter century the proportion of women having three or more children fell by 50 percent. Another way of viewing this substantial decline in childbearing is to consider that in 1976 the ratio of women ages forty to forty-four with at least three children to those who were childless was about six to one; by 2002 the ratio was less than two to one.[35] Over the same period the proportion of women having only one child by their early forties nearly doubled. Compared to the relatively few Ivy League law graduates who have traded the bar for rocking the cradle, the widespread abdication of motherhood poses an alternative question: Who is opting out of what? Women are increasingly having fewer children, and a growing proportion of women are choosing not to have any children at all. Those who do have children, Andrew Hacker points out, "are taking a new approach to motherhood. In particular, most are disinclined to make caring for their children their primary occupation."[36]

The decline in fertility and the increase in childlessness over just several decades have various implications that may or may not be seen as problematic, depending on one's perspective. From any angle, however, two issues immediately come to the fore. The first has to do with the aging of the population, which is in part a function of relatively low birthrates coupled with increasing longevity. This has created a difficulty—some would say a looming crisis—in regard to sustaining the integrity of old age pensions in the United States and throughout the advanced industrialized nations. Moreover, an aging population shrinks public interest in supporting the community infrastructure of schools, parks, and public services, which aid in the task of raising children.[37]

The second issue concerns the varying characteristics of people with different fertility rates, which have conspicuous political and cultural implications. Those having two or more children tend to be less educated, more religious, and more traditionally oriented than people with fewer than two children—and they are more likely to stand politically toward the right. In the 2004 election, George Bush took twenty-five of the twenty-six states with the highest white fertility rates, while John Kerry took the states that were least prolific.[38] Going beyond presidential elections, Phillip Longman suggests that the different fertility rates between secular individualists and religious conservatives augur a vast cultural transformation. He anticipates a resurgence of patriarchy in modern societies, which are increasingly populated by families with traditional religious values. In France, for example, although less than 33 percent of women born in the early 1960s have three or more children, "this distinct minority of French women (most of them presumably practicing Catholics and Muslims) produced more than 50 percent of all children born to their generation."[39]

Whether or not one perceives in the changing structure of family life an acute problem for old age security, a boon to the political right, or a boost to patriarchy, the demographic shift is a serious matter. Ben Wattenberg's warning about population decline in 1987 did not stir much public debate.[40] More recently, scholars and demographers, of course, have been aware of the historic decline in fertility and the aging of the population.[41] It is curious, however, that an 80 percent jump in childlessness in one generation went relatively unnoticed in the public arena compared to the media blitz accorded the 2 percent decline in women's labor-force participation. One might take this as a sign of the diminished value of motherhood in the early years of the twenty-first century. The implicit message is that work for pay is far more important than producing and caring for children—at least in the minds of many media personalities responsible for highlighting social trends.

The increasing rate of childlessness is not unique to the United States. The proportions of childless women above the age of forty in Britain, Austria, Switzerland, and Sweden are about the same as that in the United States.[42] Family size is shrinking amid declining fertility rates in the advanced industrial democracies. In the Netherlands, where the average age of first-time mothers has climbed to 29.6, demographers predict that 20 percent of the Dutch women born in 1985 will remain childless.[43] In Germany more than 25 percent of the women born in 1965 are estimated to be childless.[44] Although the U.S. fertility rate fell from 2.48 in 1970 to 2.06 in 2000, it remains higher than that of all European Union countries, among which Italy and Spain have the lowest birthrates at about 1.3.[45] Norway, with one of the highest fertility rates in Europe (1.8), is close to the United States.[46]

In addition to women having fewer children, mothers are increasingly leaving the daily care of their preschool children to other people. Between 1991 and 2001 the proportion of three-to-five-year-old children supervised by caregivers other than their parents increased from 69 to 74 percent.[47] A significant number of these children spent the better part of their days in out-of-home care. According to estimates from the Urban Institute, 41 percent of all children under five years of age whose mothers are employed are in day care for thirty-five hours a week or more. (The figure rises to 52 percent for those whose mothers work full-time.)[48] European scholars have assigned this process the cumbrous label of "defamilialization," thereby shrouding the transfer of maternal childcare from the home to the public crèche and private day-care provider in a gender-neutral veil.[49]

In addition to concealing the role of motherhood as the linchpin of family life, the veil of defamilialization obscures emerging social pressures that diminish the family's station as an institution that shelters the individual from both the state and the market. As the functions of household production and social care are surrendered to the market and the state, family members come to depend less on hearth and kin and more on external sources for their personal security and well-being. Ultimately, this reliance on the state and the market erodes the bonds of family life, leaving its members as independent actors who are free to seek their private pleasures and are constrained mainly by obligations to serve the market (as workers and consumers) and the state (as taxpayers and public employees). The coming of a new social order tends to be read from different points of view.[50] Where traditionalists see a moral decline into selfish individualism, deficient parenting, and social instability, postmodernists witness the liberation of human relations, allowing what Anthony Giddens calls "pure relationships" to flower unfettered from established conventions of habit and duty.[51] To stem the decline of child-centered family life would require, as James Q. Wilson puts it, "reversing the greatest accomplishment of the West: human emancipation."[52]

Whether or not a new social order is really in the making, the dramatic increase in childlessness—from one in ten to almost one in five women—and the rise in out-of-home care for young children does qualify as some sort of a social revolution. If women have been "opting out" of anything, the revolt against motherhood appears to be more widespread than the recent decline in labor-force participation. Still, the ebb in labor-force participation should not be dismissed too readily, as it might be the start of a sea change that ultimately reverses the tide.

Talk of a social revolution conveys a sense of fundamental change. It seems to promise a new awakening that is compelling women to substitute one type of life for another. Claims of an opt-out revolution from motherhood to the labor market or the other way around imply that all women pretty much want the same thing—whatever that may be—when it comes to career and family. Indeed, it may have looked that way in earlier times. Although the question of what women want has plagued men for ages, it became a serious matter for women only in modern times in the advanced industrial societies. Before the contraceptive revolution of the mid-1960s, biology may not have been destiny, but it certainly contributed to the childbearing fate of women who engaged in sexual activity. Up until 1965, in fact, it was illegal in Connecticut to provide information and medical advice on the use of contraceptives to married people.[53] In addition, most women needed men for their economic survival before the equal opportunity movement in the 1960s, which opened access to virtually all careers. Moreover, the expansion of white-collar jobs and jobs for secondary earners after the 1960s presented women with a viable range of employment alternatives to traditional domestic life. Taken together, these advances in contraceptive technology and civil rights along with changes in the labor market have transformed women's opportunities to control and shape their personal lives.[54]

Chapter II
Work and Family: The Choices Women Make

One way of examining the choices women make is to take family size as an indicator of the constraints and considerations that give purpose and order to their daily lives. From this perspective we can distinguish at least four general categories that form a continuum of work-family lifestyles—traditional, neotraditional, modern, and postmodern. These categories are conditioned on the number of children in the family and linked to the mainspring of personal identity from which women derive a sense of achievement in life. Women having three or more children are associated with the traditional lifestyle, two children with the neotraditional, one child with the modern, and childlessness with the postmodern way of life. The actual proportion in each category corresponds to the distribution of fertility rates among women nearing the completion of their childbearing years. In 2002, 29 percent of women ages forty to forty-four had three or more children, 35.5 percent had two children, 17.5 percent had one child, and 18 percent were childless.[1]

This classification is an ideal type in the Weberian

sense—an analytic frame that encapsulates a set of essential characteristics that distinguish a range of women's family-work lifestyles choices. The categories are logical but by no means exhaustive.[2] And as with any typology of this sort there are exceptions within every category. It helps to think of these lifestyle traits as patterns that occur usually but not always.

At one end of the continuum are women with three or more children, who are oriented toward the traditional lifestyle. These women generally derive their sense of personal identity and achievement from performing the time-honored duties of childrearing and household management. This is not to say that all "traditional" mothers assume this role for their entire lives. The number of children a woman has, their spacing, and the mother's age at the first birth will influence the length of time invested mainly in domestic life. Many of these women spend a good number of years, perhaps even the majority of their adult lives, in the paid labor force.

But they also spend a substantial period of time as stay-at-home mothers. Although traditional women are fervently engaged in childrearing, their styles of mothering may vary depending on education and background. Some mothers take pleasure in what Sharon Hays identifies as the ideology of "intensive mothering," continuously working with their children—explaining, negotiating, distracting—and scheduling a stunning array of activities.[3] Others may appear more laissez faire and create a less-structured environment, a style based on what Annette Lareau calls "accomplishment of natural growth."[4] Lareau found that this approach was followed by working-class and poor women in her sample, in contrast to the middle-class respondents whose "concerted cultivation" style of childrearing was the virtual equivalent of "intensive mothering." Although Hays maintains that all the women in her sample were devoted to the ideology of intensive mothering, in practice class differences appeared, which produced childrearing patterns that looked very similar to those found by Lareau.[5]

While their approaches to childrearing may differ, traditional mothers share an abiding belief that the daily care and socialization of their children is the most meaningful job in life. It is a job to which they are devoted full-time and from which they draw a deep sense of personal accomplishment. Even if they do not all perform the job the same way, the time and value they attribute to it and the satisfactions derived from socialization, care, and home management place this work at the center of their daily lives.

But what about gender relations? Although these women's primary duties—household management and child care—follow the traditional division of labor, it does not necessarily follow that their personal lives are constrained by the type of male-dominated gender relations associated with much of family existence prior to the 1960s. The social fabric of American life has changed considerably since that time—Archie Bunker was an anomaly even by the 1970s. The pervasive gains in women's rights and educational achievements have increased gender equality throughout society, including family life. In family relations based on a social partnership of interdependence and mutual adjustment, couples decide how to divide their labor most effectively to satisfy personal needs and family responsibilities, which does not require that all duties be split evenly down the middle.[6] Many women who choose the traditional family-work lifestyle are full partners in the joint enterprise of family life. Still, inequalities persist. It is no doubt fair to say that to the extent the hierarchy of male dominance in family life still exists, it is more likely to surface in the traditional category.

The past several decades have seen a pronounced tilt away from the traditional side of the continuum. The proportion of women with three children at the end of their childbearing years sank from 59 percent in 1976 to 29 percent in 2002. At the other end of the continuum, the number of women engaged in the postmodern lifestyle reached historic proportions as the rate of childlessness climbed to almost one in five during this same period.[7] In the past, high rates of childlessness have been attributed to intense poverty, poor nutrition, and the absence of men during wartime. But those conditions do not apply today, and modern rates of infertility do not explain the decline either.[8] Childless women are a highly individualistic, work-centered group for whom a sense of personal achievement tends to be measured by success in business, political, and intellectual life rather than in the traditional realms of motherhood. These are the women in Sylvia Ann Hewlett's sample of high-powered professionals, almost half of whom were childless at age forty. As a group they are disproportionately well educated. An analysis of the women who graduated from college in the late 1960s and early 1970s showed that 28 percent were childless in 1991, when they reached thirty-seven to forty-seven years of age; that rate climbed to 50 percent among the women who had active careers.[9]

The postmodern lifestyle corresponds to that enjoyed by a new breed of thirty-to-forty-year-old women in the United Kingdom. According to a 2004 report for Standard Life Bank, 28 percent of five hundred working women surveyed were identified as "contrasexuals"—"women of their time, who are independent minded, secure in their own company, adventurous, and confident of their own ability to handle all aspects of their lives."[10] As happy alone or in the company of friends as with a partner, these women have ambitions that are not shaped by the prospects of marriage and family life. Indeed, one of the survey's most revealing findings was that less than half of the working women interviewed said that having a family and creating a happy home environment would give them the greatest sense of fulfillment in life. Almost 40 percent of these women attributed the greatest sense of fulfillment in life to an extraordinary personal achievement (such as climbing a mountain or learning to fly a plane), to success in their professional life, and to staying slim, fit, and healthy.

One might wonder why Standard Life Bank was involved in a study of women who were shunning marriage and families in favor of the good life. It was not entirely a matter of sociological curiosity. Another prominent characteristic of the contrasexuals is that, in contrast to the other working women, they are more likely to go off on adventurous vacations as well as more inclined to take out mortgages and purchase their own homes (and use their mortgage to finance their vacations). Of the 19 percent who had a mortgage on their own, more than half of them said they would keep the mortgage and property for as long as possible, even if they met a partner and wanted to settle down. Thus, the contrasexuals represent not only a lifestyle but a growing market for mortgage brokers and refinance specialists. A similar pattern is found in the United States, where 21 percent of all homes sold in 2005 were sold to single women—up from 10 percent twenty years earlier.[11]

In the middle of the continuum are the neotraditional and modern women who have either one or two children. These women are interested in paid work, but they are not so thoroughly committed to a career that they would forego motherhood. Although a bare majority, they are often seen as representative of all women, especially those who are trying to "have it all." In balancing the demands of employment and family, women with one child normally tip the scales in favor of their careers, while those with two children lean more toward domestic life. Both groups vary in degrees from the traditional and the postmodern lifestyles. To the extent that women are opting out of the labor market to stay home and raise their children, they are most likely to come from these two groups—joining traditional mothers who are already outside the labor market.

The neotraditional group contains families with two children whose mothers are likely to be employed—often part-time—but are physically and emotionally more invested in their home life than their jobs. Since 1976 the proportion of women over age forty with only two children has increased by 75 percent and currently amounts to about 35 percent of the women in that age group. The modern family usually involves a working mother with one child; these women are more career-oriented and devote greater time and energy to their paid employment than neotraditional women. The proportion of women over forty with only one child has climbed by almost 90 percent since 1976 and currently amounts to 17 percent of the women in this age group.

As general types, the traditional, neotraditional, modern, and postmodern categories help draw attention to the diversity of work and family choices as well as to how the size of these groups has shifted over the past three decades. Ideal types are like impressionist paintings: they portray sufficient dimensions of a category to evoke meaning, but the borders are fuzzy and porous. So, to repeat, in each group there are women who do not fit the ideal type—childless women who do not work and women with three or more children who are employed full-time. Also, accident, illness, divorce, poor timing, and plain bad luck may have hampered lifestyle choices for some, so in each group there are women who might have wanted to be in another category. Finally as people live and learn, there is movement among the categories. Women may start out their adult lives oriented more toward either having careers or rearing children and later change their minds and lifestyles.

Certainly, there are some women who would rather have additional children and not go to work but are financially compelled out of dire necessity to participate in the labor force and have fewer children. For most people in the United States, however, I would argue that what is often considered economic "necessity" amounts to a preferred level of material comfort—home ownership, automobiles, vacations, cell phones, DVDs, and the like. The triumph of materialism in modern times feeds the market and leaves childrearing and family life undernourished. This point, of course, is highly debatable and will be taken up in greater detail in Chapter 4. For the moment let us accept that the trade-off between higher levels of material consumption and a more traditional domestic life is largely a matter of individual choice.

Wants or Preferences?

Beginning in the 1960s, women's capacity to exercise choice in regard to family size was dramatically advanced by opportunities to control procreation through modern contraception, legalized abortion, and assisted reproductive technology. At the same time their options regarding labor-force participation increased. These developments created new alternatives for women in the realms of work and family life, which led to changes in family size and patterns of employment. Women now have fewer children and work outside the home more than in the past. This realignment of family-work lifestyles raises a question: Does the current distribution among traditional, neotraditional, modern, and postmodern arrangements accurately reflect women's genuine lifestyle preferences? Social scientists offer at least three cautious answers to this question— "no, not exactly," "yes, pretty much," and "too soon to tell."

Reflecting the negative assessment, Hewlett notes that for the most part the high-achieving women she studied did not choose to be childless and, indeed, yearned for children.[12] This observation is common. Various surveys have shown that many women who are childless would have preferred otherwise. According to Gallup polls conducted in 1990 and 2003, for example, 62 to 70 percent of the respondents over age forty who did not have children indicated that they would prefer to have at least one child (and more than half of them said two children) if they had it to do over again.[13] The U.S. Census Bureau reported that between 1976 and 1992 women's average birth expectations remained fairly constant at 2.1 children. Among women ages eighteen to thirty-four in 1992 only 9 percent expected to have no births in their lifetime, yet the rate of childlessness among women over forty years of age in 2002 was almost double that amount.[14] According to Sharon Hays, when asked "how you would feel if you never had children," many of the mothers in her study expressed despondency. "Nearly one-quarter of the women I talked to actually cried when I asked them this question," Hays reported. "And the answers of nearly all mothers—'lonely,' 'empty,' 'missing something'—were stunningly consistent."[15]

As for women's inclinations toward mixing paid work and family life, public opinion polls show that significant percentages of women would prefer not to work at all outside the home or not to engage in full-time employment. In response to a nationwide Gallup survey in 1980, for example, 55 percent of the women who wanted to be married and have children did not wish to have a full-time job or career outside the home.[16] The Virginia Slims surveys conducted between 1974 and 1989 convey wavering inclinations toward paid employment and family life. Asked what they would prefer if free to choose, 36 percent of the women in 1974 said they would rather have jobs than stay at home and care for the family; the proportion favoring this choice increased to 52 percent in 1985 but then declined to 42 percent in 1989.[17] According to the 1997 Survey of American Families, 49 percent of women respondents agreed with the statement "When children are young mothers should not work outside the home."[18] This view is supported by women's responses to many surveys in the 1990s.[19]

Numerous polls show women articulating ideals and favoring choices about family size, child care, and work that do not exactly coincide with the outcomes expressed in their behavior regarding these matters. But should we take these results to mean that the 2002 distributions of family size and home care do not reflect what women really want? Before answering we should recall an old saw in survey research: "Tell me the answer you like and I'll write the question." When faced with life's many choices, the desire to have children and care for them at home may be real and strong, but at a given moment it may not be quite as strong as other desires. One might want to have three children, a large house, a high-status career, and a small yacht to sail around on when not working, minding the kids, or taking care of the house. But if it is not possible to obtain all of these worldly delights simultaneously, which come first?

In most of the surveys examined here, wants are not disciplined by preferences. Preferences are wants ordered according-ing to how much they are favored at the time choices have to be made. Do you want a yacht? Yes, indeed, very much. What about a large house? Yes. If you had enough money to purchase only one, which would it be? And would you put off both purchases, along with the high-paying career necessary to pay for them, until after you've had and raised the three children you want? And so it goes. Although surveys have consistently shown the average ideal family size to be around 2.5 children, many women in their twenties and thirties faced with the real-life choice between working and raising two or more children may *want* the latter but have increasingly expressed a *preference* for work.

Surveys about what women want in the way of work and family do not address the ultimate question of how satisfied they are with the choices they finally make. On this score, an analysis of nationally representative data from the General Social Survey during the period from 1994 to 2004 reveals that 62 percent of married, stay-at-home mothers age forty-five and under reported being "very happy" in their marriages compared to 53 percent for those mothers in the same age category who were employed full-time. By contrast, more than 74 percent of childless wives age forty-five and under reported being "very happy" in their marriages, whether they stayed at home or were employed outside. But the most important determinant of marital happiness had less to do with women's labor-force participation than with the emotional engagement of their husbands.[20]

Self-reports of marital happiness, of course, are subject to the same caveats that apply to social surveys reporting on what women want. Reported levels of happiness in marital life do not exactly square with the modern probability of divorce. Taking a somewhat jaundiced view of the enterprise, Laura

Kipnis suggests that in light of the current divorce rate, "all indications are that whomever you love today—the center of your universe, your little Poopsie—has a good chance of becoming your worst nightmare at least 50 percent of the time." She goes on to note that the percentage includes only those who actually leave unhappy unions and does not factor in the happiness (or unhappiness) level of all those who remain married.[21]

Those who argue that women have gotten pretty much what they most want would claim that survey responses ultimately amount to a lot of talk about the things women *might* want. When it comes to action, however, the choices women make effectively express their genuine preferences regarding family and work, and these preferences vary. Thus, modern women supposedly have taken full measure of the physical, psychological, and spiritual joys of motherhood and decided that one child is enough. For them the added love and emotional satisfaction of a second and third child—the marginal utility, as it were—are judged insufficient to warrant the costs. Traditional and neotraditional women express different predispositions, which favor having families of two and three or more children.

As for women who are childless, Catherine Hakim cites a burgeoning literature that shows them to be sexually active, often married, and disproportionately well educated; childlessness can no longer be explained as a misfortune imposed by social isolation, poverty, or illness. The literature suggests that there are two groups who choose not to have children: "those who reject the advantages of children—who usually decide early—and those who are not prepared to lose the advantages of a childfree lifestyle—who usually decide late." Hakim concludes, "Voluntary childlessness also refutes the idea that all women have a natural or instinctive desire for motherhood."[22] From this perspective motherhood is less of a biological imperative than a preferred lifestyle choice.

Postmodern women, for whom the optimal lifestyle involves no children, see themselves as *childfree* rather than *childless.* They extoll the virtues of a life unencumbered by diapers, running noses, incessant chatter, and endless anxiety. Those who enjoy the pleasures of a childfree lifestyle usually agree with the ironic "musings of a good father on a bad day" published in one of Ann Landers's columns, particularly the last few lines: "The childless couple live in a vacuum. They fill their lonely days with golf, vacation trips, dinner dates, civic affairs, tranquility, leisure and entertainment. There is a terrifying emptiness without children, but the childless couple are too comfortable to know it. You just have to look at them to see what the years have done: He looks boyish, unlined and rested; she's slim, well-groomed and youthful. It isn't natural. If they had had kids, they'd look like the rest of us—worn out, wrinkled and exhausted."[23]

Since the early 1990s, as some organizations have tried to become more "family friendly," concern has been expressed that flextime policies and other workplace accommodations for working mothers discriminate against childfree women, who are often tapped to stay late when a deadline must be met and to take up the slack when working parents have a family emergency or just need to leave early to pick up their children. One complaint is that family-friendly benefits, based solely on procreation, often serve the interests of working mothers in the middle and professional classes. Eligibility for these benefits is established according to lifestyle choices rather than financial need or unavoidable hardships.[24] Advocates for childfree women see them as victims not of infertility but of other women who have chosen to procreate. This view challenges the notion that women's interests are dominated by the common struggle to surmount biological determinism, patriarchal socialization, financial dependence on men, and workplace discrimination. In many ways women who are childfree have fundamentally different needs and interests than working mothers.

Following in this vein, Hakim's "preference theory" maintains that women do not form an essentially homogenous group in which everyone seeks to combine work and family life. Preference theory posits that there is an unyielding tension between a life centered on family—meeting the continuous demands of marriage, childrearing, and household management—and a life centered on paid employment and meeting the continuous demands of a full-time career (while attending to household necessities). In responding to this tension, Hakim argues, women have distinct predispositions that bear on how much their personal identity and sense of achievement derives from paid work in the market and how much from investments in family life. It is not clear, however, how these predispositions are formed or the extent to which they are amenable to change. Unable to find any systematic relations between women's lifestyle choices and individual characteristics such as ability and education, Hakim concludes that "there is no single factor that determines or explains why women differ so significantly in their preferences."[25]

Thus, on the one hand, a reading of public opinion polls and various case studies reveals a serious challenge to the notion that over the past three decades the changing distribution among traditional, neotraditional, modern, and postmodern lifestyles accurately reflects what women really want (although a critical reading of these sources casts some doubts on their implications). On the other hand, preference theory tells us that because women in advanced industrialized democracies such as the United States have greater freedom than ever before to decide how much time and effort to devote to paid employment and childrearing activities, the lifestyles they have chosen are pretty much what they prefer. (One might demur, however, that preference theory does not so much explain behavior as describe it and then attribute what has been found to innate preferences, which are malleable to varying degrees.)

Innate Desires or Transient Tendencies?

The final answer is that we really do not yet know whether women's choices regarding paid work and childrearing over the past several decades represent a transient phase that is due for a correction, or whether they represent a basic pattern of deep-seated lifestyle preferences that will continue over time. Yet, my hunch is that the distribution of choices regarding motherhood and employment over this period is not an accurate representation of genuine lifestyle preferences. I think that the distribution of lifestyle choices is distorted by an asymmetrical knowledge of the supposed value of each option and by incomplete information about the range of alternatives. By that I mean that the choices have been influenced by a one-sided view of the costs of having children and the benefits of shifting labor from the household to the market, and that at the same time these choices have been narrowed by a limited perspective on the possibilities for harmonizing work and family life.

There are several reasons for this point of view. To begin with, I am not sure we know how well women's choices reflect a pattern of deep-seated preferences, because it is still too early in the contemporary game of changing lifestyles. Also, just as women are finding more possibilities for work and education, they are also facing a longer lifespan within which to realize these options. Ronald Lee and Joshua Goldstein suggest that young people today are beginning to internalize the likelihood of living into their nineties. As these extra years of life are factored in, Lee and Goldstein see a "rescaling of the life cycle" that includes delaying marriage and childbirth, moving back home after college, and prolonging adolescence.[26]

Since the 1960s men and women have been learning about the implications of their work and family choices—and the current generation may now be reordering their preferences and rescaling their investments of time based on experience. Preference theory would suggest that the professional women shown to be opting out of the market probably had a strong inherent predisposition toward a more traditional lifestyle but were temporarily seduced by what appeared to be glamorous, rewarding work—until the biological clock began to sound an alarm or until the first child arrived, arousing their innate maternal preferences. Maybe for some of them, after a few years on the job, what appeared to be glamorous, rewarding work to a twenty-one-year-old turned out to be monotonous and wearing by age twenty-seven. Others may have decided to postpone the corporate or professional climb until another day—accepting the likelihood that a late start would reduce the chances of getting to the top.

At the same time there are women who may have wanted two or more children but delayed having the first child until they completed their education, established themselves in professional life, and got married—at which point it was too late to have a second child (and in some cases, perhaps, even the first). Indeed, since the 1970s, there has been a growing discrepancy between the accuracy with which women anticipate their future patterns of work and family life. At the end of the 1970s about 80 percent of women in their late teens envisioned their future participation in the labor force. By the time they were thirty-five years old their actual participation rate was about 75 percent. For this generation it appears that women's life experiences matched their expectations about work more closely than their expectations about family life. Among women in their freshman year of college during that time, 82 percent expected to have children; by the time they were thirty-seven years old, only 69 percent actually had a child.[27]

Within the span of a single decade, from the early 1970s to the early 1980s, the median age of marriage for college-educated women shot up by 2.5 years, from 22.5 to 25 years old.[28] This might not sound like much, but if we consider eighteen as the age of emancipation, the additional years before marriage represent a more than 50 percent increase in the period of time college-educated women live as independent, single adults. The average age of mothers having their first child in the United States has climbed during the past several decades from 21.4 years old in 1970 to almost 25 years in 2000.[29] The average age of first-time mothers in most of Europe is reported as 30 years old.[30] The average age may rise or fall as social learning about the implications of postponed marriage and childbearing occurs. As the current generation of women in their twenties and early thirties consider rescaling the life cycle, they will no doubt examine and learn from their parents' experience.

Another reason that I think the lifestyle choices may be due for a correction is that social class, income, and the type of work available to people inevitably influence the attractions of family and work. Some women can opt out of their careers while still maintaining a very comfortable material standard of living. And some simply must work to support their families. Others may be persuaded to work by strong prospects for engaging in prestigious, empowering, flexible, and interesting careers. The latter group must weigh the social and economic trade-offs of working in the labor force against staying home with their children in the context of realistically anticipating access to highly satisfying and meaningful work. These women are influenced not only by income but by the kind of work they would expect to be doing to earn the income. Some jobs are simply more enjoyable than others, and that factor likely feeds into any woman's decision-making process. In addition, the emerging pattern of lifestyle choices may respond to changes in the character of working life, but the direction and impact of these changes are not yet clear. Increased telecommuting and part-time employment, for example, might soften the demands of working life by enhancing the flexibility of weekly schedules and the opportunity to spend more time at home. Yet one could also envision the mounting competitive pressures from low-wage developing countries in a global economy resulting in a more callused workplace. As Lucy Kellaway claimed in 2006, "The increasing talk of work-life balance has gone hand in hand with more work and less life. The term is still routinely used but has lost its resonance and in 2007 it will start to sicken and die."[31]

Finally, I would suggest that the pattern of choices in recent decades has been distorted by the conventional discourse on balancing work and family life, which has been framed for the most part in such a way as to discount, if not entirely ignore, certain alternatives. The standard choices have been posed as having a number of children and staying home to care for them; having few or no children and making paid employment the central activity of life; and trying to create a balance (often referred to as "harmonizing") between production in the market and reproduction at home, which usually involves some combination of full-time work, part-time work, flexible work schedules, and varying amounts of out-of-home child care. These alternatives take as axiomatic that "going to work" or "having a career" means doing what men usually do—that is, entering the labor force immediately after completing their education and remaining there with nose to the grindstone until the age of retirement. Other alternatives have been faintly voiced, such as the idea that work and family life might be balanced not by juggling them at the same time but by engaging in each separately for a varying number of years over the long course of modern life. In recent years, however, the voices seem to be getting louder, not so much in the established circles of feminist academic and political leadership as among the rank and file of the coming generation of college women, many of whom are trying to imagine how to achieve the right balance for a satisfying life.

Not only are some alternatives scarcely articulated, but there is an imbalance in the social support for those that are most commonly expressed. In any society, individuals' lifestyle choices can be skewed by overbearing cultural constraints or government dictates, such as the social and religious conventions against women working in some Muslim countries or the one-child policy in China. Such forceful normative demands and exacting regulatory strictures do not apply in the United States; however, although they are less prescriptive, the prevailing norms and values, as well as policy incentives that reinforce those norms and values, do have a strong effect. They influence how people perceive lifestyle alternatives, the worth attributed to these alternatives, and the behavior that follows. In the 1960s, for example, widely shared expectations and values assured that cohabitation and openly gay unions were rarely practiced outside of bohemian venues. Today, the formerly dodgy customs of North Beach and Greenwich Village have migrated into the mainstream of almost every major city and college town in the United States.

It is evident that the highly personal lifestyle choices of women concerning how to balance work and childrearing are not made in a vacuum. They are influenced by each individual's particular circumstances—the sum of health, wealth, and providence—as well as by the social pressures of norms and values in a given cultural context. My interests lie in examining how capitalism, feminism, and the state contribute to these cultural norms and values and how the social pressures they generate influence lifestyle choices and the changing role of motherhood. In the United States, the twenty-first-century culture of capitalism influences how we value household labor and assess the costs and benefits of childrearing. The prevailing strains of feminist ideology communicate normative expectations about the extent to which work and children constitute the basic ingredients of a psychologically and emotionally satisfying life for modern women. The state, through publicly financed family-friendly policies, creates incentives and legitimates work-and-family lifestyle choices, which reinforce the social influences of capitalism and feminism. In the following chapters I will take a critical look at the nature of these capitalist values, habits of mind, and feminist expectations, and how they support the various lifestyle choices of women trying to reconcile the demands of childrearing and work.

II
Capitalism, Feminism, and the Family-Friendly State

Chapter III
Capitalism and Motherhood: Does It Pay to Have Children?

Before looking into the influence of capitalism on motherhood, let us begin with an age-old question: Can capitalism survive? Karl Marx, as we all know, thought not. He claimed that ever-increasing competition and the drive for profit would intensify the exploitation of labor, sharpening class conflict and triggering the inevitable downfall of capitalism.[1] Responding to this question almost a century after the publication of the *Communist Manifesto,* the well-known economic theorist Joseph Schumpeter agreed with Marx that capitalism was doomed, but not because it produced misery and heightened exploitation. On the contrary, he saw capitalism as delivering unprecedented material benefits and a higher standard of life for all classes—and his paradoxical thesis was that "capitalism is being killed by its achievements."[2]

Schumpeter outlined several reasons for believing that the capitalist order would self-destruct.[3] First, he argued that as the capitalist engine of productivity generated goods and services and lifted the social and economic conditions of all classes, it lowered the special social and political powers of the business class. Moreover, by increasing the general standard of living, amount of leisure time, and educational opportunities for the masses, and by bringing down the costs of newspapers, books, and radios (television was not yet a common commodity, even among the rich), capitalism cultivated a seedbed for the rise of an independent intellectual class. Although their standards and interests would eventually become hostile to those of large-scale business, once unloosed in society the intellectual class cannot be brought to heel. Finally, he believed that the capitalist ethos inculcated rational habits of the mind, leading individuals to calculate life's choices through a cost-benefit lens framed by utilitarian ends. Ironically, he argued, this rationalization of human behavior sapped the vitality of the very family and social values that originally animated the capitalist spirit and sparked entrepreneurial activity.[4]

Schumpeter saw the disintegration of capitalist society already under way in the late 1930s as the capitalist order was breached by the introduction of widely accepted public interventions in the market economy. He interpreted government regulatory measures, progressive taxation, social security legislation and other public provisions for welfare (which laid the foundation for modern welfare states) as signaling the march into socialism.[5]

Schumpeter's Error

For now, and as far down the road as we can see, history has proved Schumpeter wrong on several accounts. As the intellectual class evolved, it was not immune to the capitalist culture of innovation, competition, and choice. Thriving on disagreement, intellectuals generated a competitive marketplace of ideas in which critical perceptions of capitalism vie with analyses that proclaim its virtues.[6] By the dawn of the twenty-first century, politically Left-leaning foundations, periodicals, and think tanks in the United States had been well met by the rise of alternative institutes on the Right. Indeed, it has been argued that in recent years the brigades of idea-generating agents on the Right have forcefully influenced the public agenda.[7] Not only do the publications of the intellectual class express varying political orientations, but occasionally their positions change over time. Nathan Glazer tells, for example, of how a popular policy journal that began with a liberal tilt drifted to the Right as submissions reflected the increasing energy and powerful ideas generated by conservative think tanks and foundations.[8]

Rather than undermining the capitalist order, the growth of modern welfare states has shored it up by ameliorating some of the personal costs and insecurities associated with a competitive private market. Indeed, there is credible evidence that since the early 1980s, government-supported institutions of social welfare have quietly shifted from offering programs and benefits geared toward meeting citizens' needs to advancing welfare reforms designed to serve the needs of the private market.[9] Throughout the advanced industrialized countries, unemployment, disability, and social-assistance programs originally intended to protect labor have morphed into schemes to promote work. While forging tight links between benefits and work-related activities, the objectives of recent reforms have been wrapped in a discourse of "activation" (seriously looking for work), "social inclusion" (joining the paid labor force), and "responsibility" (achieving financial independence). The active-inclusive-responsible aspirations of the current discourse smoothly dispense with the initial objectives of income maintenance and social protection against the vicissitudes of life in capitalist society.[10] In more forthright terms, these reforms are usually described as a shift from welfare to "workfare."

Along with the advent of workfare, social programs have increasingly come to embrace the market-oriented standards of privatization and choice.[11] The Swedish social democratic welfare-state model is often considered the progressive standard for publicly supported social protection. In the early 1990s, however, a system of educational vouchers was introduced in Sweden under which parents who chose to send their children to private schools were entitled to receive a voucher equivalent to 85 percent of the cost of a public education; the value was lowered to 75 percent in 1994. A few years later, the Swedish pension system underwent sweeping reforms, including a measure that allowed taxpayers to invest almost 14 percent of their total contributions to the public system in private individual reserve accounts. According to Mauricio Rojas, a member of the Swedish parliament, this measure "has turned the Swedish people into one of the most capitalist societies in the world, creating an atypical popular interest in the stock market's ups and downs."[12] Sweden's partial privatization of pensions is not exceptional. Since 1992 thirty countries have incorporated private individual accounts into their mandatory pension systems, including Denmark, the United Kingdom, Italy, Poland, Slovakia, and Hungary.[13]

More generally, instead of capitalist societies marching into socialism as Schumpeter predicted, the reverse is happening. The socialist countries of Eastern Europe have flocked from command economies to capitalist-inspired free-market economies. Even in China, which is still firmly in the political grip of the Communist Party, the shift toward what they now call "market socialism" is well under way. Between 1990 and

2003, private firms rapidly increased as the number of employees in state-owned enterprises plunged by 33 percent.[14]

Time has not confirmed Schumpeter's bold and provocative forecast of the triumph of socialism.[15] As capitalism thrives, however, his analysis of how it contributes to the deterioration of traditional family values remains all the more compelling—and is of particular interest to our inquiry into the impact of social values on women's lifestyle choices. But what has the status of family life to do with the rise or fall of capitalism? Schumpeter perceived an intimate connection between the bonds of family life and the entrepreneurial spirit. Family bonds reinforced a future-oriented perspective, which encouraged the kind of planning and discipline that kindled entrepreneurial behavior. According to this view, children, in particular, inspire parents to sacrifice material pleasures of the moment in order to save and invest for the future. Children introduce a utilitarian calculus to adult behavior that is at odds with the rational self-interest of childless adults whose worldview is not filtered through the nursery-room windows of a family home.

According to Schumpeter, the absence of children deprives business leaders of the motivation to construct a sturdy roof of economic security to shelter the family line. Without the need and desire to provide for the next generation, the businessman "might be less willing than he was to fulfill the function of earning, saving, and investing even if he saw no reason to fear that the results would but swell his tax bills." If the decline of family life indeed diminishes a motivating force of entrepreneurial behavior, then the low birthrates and rising number of childless marriages in the 1930s would have posed a serious problem.[16] Writing in the summer of 1935, Schumpeter maintained that the capitalist order was being jeopardized by the attenuation of the family unit (he allowed, however, that the bourgeois family still tenaciously clung to life). Although the rising number of childless marriages after World War I was reversed by the resurgence of familism after World War II, the sinking birth and marriage rates since the mid-1960s lend credibility to his observations.

Feeding the Market

What Schumpeter's analysis failed to detect was that the deterioration of traditional family life in many ways nurtures the market economy (at least once the engines of capitalist productivity were primed). Along with the decline in marriage, increasing levels of cohabitation, and the rise in childlessness, by the dawn of the twenty-first century the traditional arrangement of mothers at home and fathers in the paid labor force represented only 29 percent of all married couples—down by one-third from 1980. But these trends hardly undermined the capitalist order. More than anything else, perhaps, today's affluent capitalist societies require a flexible labor force and extravagant consumption of the ever-expanding supply of modern luxuries. Whether advertising incites consumers to want often trivial stuff that adds little to the quality of life, as John Galbraith argued, or whether it just provides us with knowledge about what is being produced, as Friedrich Hayek responded, capitalism has a way of turning luxuries into what people consider to be necessities.[17]

For both luxuries and necessities, single people are terrific consumers. Contrasexuals want to take flying lessons and yoga classes; they purchase their own condos and refinance the mortgage to go scuba diving off the Ivory Coast; and, without ties to partners and children, they constitute a highly mobile labor force. Childless couples, known as DINKs (dual-income, no kids), are slightly less mobile but tend to have more surplus income for purchasing homes, snappy clothes, the latest in flat-screen TVs, and mountain bikes, and for enjoying nights out on the town together. High rates of divorce have created an industry of mediators, therapists, and family lawyers; promoted real estate sales and day-care services; and increased the labor-force participation of women. Two-income married couples with children rely heavily on a support network of fast-food vendors, dry cleaners, housekeeping services, personal time organizers, gardeners, and nannies and other child-care providers.

In addition, the unraveling of marriage and traditional family life has had some curious side effects on patterns of consumption. For example, as marriage rates fall and the practice of cohabitation becomes increasingly common, those who walk down the aisle together do so amid increasingly elaborate and expensive ceremonies. Between 1998 and 2003 the average price of weddings in England and Wales rose by 45 percent. So why are couples spending more on weddings just as marriage seems to be going out of fashion?

According to *The Economist,* it may have to do with rise in average age at which people get married. Middle-class women delay marriage to invest in their careers and raise their value on the marriage market. A lavish wedding is one way to demonstrate the increased value attached to the participants.[18] But I prefer an alternative explanation that draws more on the social-emotional meaning of the wedding event than the status attributes of conspicuous consumption. There was a time when the wedding ceremony typically marked a profound change in the daily routine of the participating couples—altering their social, emotional, and sexual lives. Not only did they sleep together for the first time that evening, but the next day they awoke to a life in which they would now be sharing the same space, enjoying sexual intimacy, and seeing each other every morning and evening. Under those circumstances, even if the wedding were a simple affair, its social implications were staggering. Today, with many couples marrying later in life and cohabiting for long periods before walking down the aisle, the event has lost much of its social consequence—following the ceremony, nothing much is altered in the couple's daily routine. Under these circumstances, perhaps, a grand wedding is an effort to lend social gravity to an otherwise unremarkable event.[19]

Another unintended consequence of the decline of family life stems from the outsourcing of household production, which accompanied the rising rates of women's labor-force participation. Inas Rashad and Michael Grossman report that as much as two-thirds of the increase in adult obesity can be explained by the explosive growth in the number of fast food restaurants per capita since 1980. "As nonwork time for women became increasingly scarce and valuable over the last few decades," Rashad and Grossman explain, "time devoted to at-home meal preparation decreased. Families began eating out more often."[20] Other researchers have found a relationship between the number of hours mothers spend in paid employment and obesity among children.[21]

In a sense Schumpeter foresaw the outsourcing of family production in his analysis of capitalism as an evolutionary process of "creative destruction." In this process the existing modes of production must endlessly compete with new commodities, new sources of supply, and new types of organization, which command a decisive cost or quality advantage. It is not so much price and quality competition among firms as the continuous cycle of new markets, new products, and new organizational developments that "revolutionizes the economic structure from within, incessantly destroying the old one, incessantly creating a new one."[22]

Although Schumpeter's discussion of creative destruction focused on industrial life, it readily applies to the outsourcing of family production. Fast-food chains, ready-made meals, and microwave ovens compete with homemade meals that have become increasingly inconvenient and relatively more expensive to prepare as women spend more time working in paid careers. Nationwide, child-care industries are launched to serve the burgeoning market for nonmaternal care of children. New reproductive technologies have created a private fertility market for renting wombs at $10,000 and purchasing eggs at a going rate of somewhere between $2,500 and $50,000. Since the start of commercial sperm banks in 1970 the commerce of conception has grown into a $3 billion industry.[23] As the boundaries between family life and the market economy soften, the capitalist process of creative destruction has moved into the productive and reproductive functions of motherhood.

The idiom "creative destruction" suggests a favorable outcome—otherwise it would not be creative. However, it is worth considering what is lost in this process. When applied to commercial life, the destruction strikes less-efficient, less-useful, old-fashioned and more-expensive modes of production. In the domain of family life, the destructive consequences extend beyond the material arena of commerce into the psychological realms of human interaction and emotional bonds.

If the creative destruction of capitalist culture subverts the bonds of domesticity, socialist doctrine is equally inhospitable to family life. "This body of thought," Irving Kristol observes, "has always been hostile to the family as an institution, not only because the family is *the* crucial vehicle for the transmission of values, but because it is in the family that the very sense of tradition, the basic human instinct of piety toward an ancestral past, is preserved and conveyed."[24] It might also be added that the family is the primary institutional vehicle through which privilege is transferred from one generation to the next. In quest of a more egalitarian, utopian society, socialism seeks a break not only with tradition but with bourgeois family life, which is depicted by Karl Marx and Friedrich Engels as exploitive—to put it mildly. In their view, "the bourgeois claptrap about the family and education, about the hallowed co-relation of parent and child, becomes all the more disgusting, the more, by the actions of modern industry, all family ties among the proletarians are torn asunder and their children transformed into simple articles of commerce and instruments of labor." In the bourgeois family, Marx and Engels claim, the wife is treated as a prostitute and a "mere instrument of production."[25] These antagonistic views of the family found practical expression when the Bolsheviks first came to power and introduced liberal reforms under which abortion and divorce rates soared. Later the laws were revised to reinforce marriage and family life.[26]

Although the bitter animosity expressed by Marx and Engels toward the family does not represent the sentiments of modern social-democratic governments, these governments do share the communists' quest for a more egalitarian society as reflected in their spirited support of family-friendly policies. In this case the equality sought is not so much among social classes as between men and women—representing the triumph of feminism over socialism. As Alan Carlson puts it, "The equality of households, the democratic socialist goal in the early twentieth century when issues of economic equity predominated, became subordinate in their scheme to the equality of individuals within households."[27] Thus, for example, by assuming traditional obligations of the biological family, a major objective of the collective "people's home" (as the Swedish state welfare is known) is to free women to participate equally with men in the labor market. In what some would consider an ironic twist, the triumph of feminism winds up advancing the culture of capitalism.

While Schumpeter may have overestimated the extent to which the fraying values and motives of traditional family life would deplete capitalist initiatives, his prediction that the material success and utilitarian conventions of capitalism would contribute to the thinning of family bonds has indeed come to pass in modern times. His line of reasoning is summed up in one very long sentence: "As soon as men and women learn the utilitarian lesson and refuse to take for granted the traditional arrangements that their social environment makes for them, as soon as they acquire the habit of weighing the individual advantages and disadvantages of any prospective course of action—or, as we might also put it, as soon as they introduce into their private lives a sort of inarticulate cost accounting—they cannot fail to become aware of the heavy personal sacrifices that family ties and especially parenthood entail under modern conditions and of the fact that at the same time, except in the cases of farmers and peasants, children cease to be economic assets."[28]

There is probably some truth in Schumpeter's claim that traditional values and conventions of family life are destabilized under capitalism. On one side, a cost-benefit mentality harnessed to the constant flow of new products feeds and arouses new desires, which disturb established conventions. On the other side, rational calculations in the quest for efficiency and material gain inculcate a mental attitude that eventually extends to the rationalization of everything in life, including social contacts and family affairs—what some have called the "commercialization of social relations."[29]

Cost-benefit calculations that inform the design of social policies related to family life can sometimes go astray. The Constitutional Court in Germany, for example, ruled in 2004 that childless workers had to start making higher contributions than those with children to the country's compulsory nursing home insurance. The reasoning behind this ruling was that parents bear the primary costs of raising the next generation of workers, who will contribute to the pay-as-you-go pension scheme, while those who are childless will reap some of the benefit when they retire.[30] Here the cost-benefit equation weighs the financial costs and ignores all of the transcendental benefits of parenthood and childrearing. Childless workers might have reversed the equation, arguing that they are the ones owed compensation since, through taxes, they bear some of the costs of free education and health care services consumed by children, but they reap none of the psychological and emotional joys of parenthood.

Another example comes from a family-friendly measure recently introduced in France that raises the question: Would you have a third child for $11,000? It is a question French officials might have pondered longer before announcing plans to increase fertility rates by awarding more than $900 a month for one year of unpaid leave from work to parents who have a third child. By trying to increase the proportion of families with three children, the new policy automatically rewards all the people who would have had large families in any case. From what we know about social characteristics related to family size, this group is likely to be less educated and more religiously orthodox, and to contain a higher proportion of immigrants than families with one child or no children. As for those who might be swayed by the offer, it is not hard to imagine that many who would find the short-term material gain a compelling motive for a long-term commitment to parenthood may not be exactly the kind of people best suited for the role.

Family Division of Labor: A Rational Choice?

Schumpeter was disturbed by the idea of subjecting parenthood to modern cost-benefit analysis because, as he saw it, the resulting balance sheet was incomplete, if not fundamentally wrong, especially when it came to the benefits of motherhood. He explained that "the contribution made by parenthood to physical and moral health—to 'normality' as we might express it—particularly in the case of women, almost invariably escapes the rational searchlight of modern individuals who, in private as in public life, tend to focus attention on ascertainable details of immediate utilitarian relevance and to sneer at the idea of hidden necessities of human nature or of the social organism."[31] The trade-off for women between rearing children in a traditional family home and living a childfree postmodern lifestyle, in other words, involves a calculated choice in which everything that counts is rarely counted accurately.

Capitalist activity inculcates a cost-benefit mind-set that poses a knotty problem for calculating choices that affect many aspects of family life, particularly childrearing activities that hinge on voluntary sacrifice and altruistic behavior. To what extent does the rational-choice approach explain family decisions, and how does it account for the "hidden" benefits, which Schumpeter perceived as being outside the purview of rational calculations based on ascertainable details of immediate utilitarian relevance? Or do hidden benefits even exist? Nobel Prize–winning economist Gary Becker's systematic application of economic analysis to the hard choices faced by family members offers some interesting insights—and raises some additional questions.[32]

According to rational choice, the traditional division of labor has been widely adopted because it offers a highly efficient way for most people to achieve their family objectives, by drawing on the comparative advantages of both men and women. These comparative advantages stem in part from specialized investments made by men and women, and in part from intrinsic differences between the sexes, particularly surrounding the reproductive process.[33] (The relationship between biology and human nature is a veritable minefield, through which Becker deftly maneuvers on the bland vernacular of comparative advantage, specialized investments, marginal utility, and an arcane array of algebraic equations.) On a good day, men's biological contribution to the production of children may involve twenty minutes or so of physically pleasurable activity. Women, on the other hand, carry and grow the fetus for nine months, endure the risks and severities of childbirth, and produce milk to nurture the child once it is born. In terms of sheer time and physical effort invested, the differences are incomparable. Thus, it is reasonable to expect that the substantial investment by women would make them more prone than men to devote themselves to the care of their children.

Biology not only encourages women to go to greater lengths in ensuring their high investment in reproduction, it also affords a comparative advantage after childbirth when, for example, the sound of an infant's crying releases oxytocin into its mother's bloodstream, stimulating the flow of her breast milk.[34] There are numerous benefits associated with breastfeeding, from lower rates of pneumonia and meningitis in children to lower rates of cancer and osteoporosis in mothers. Women are more responsive to their infants' usual crying than men (though both are equally attentive to cries of extreme distress).[35] But while women's comparative advantage may be strong, it is not absolute. In practice, less than half of all infants are breastfed, and only 18.5 percent are breastfed for at least six months.[36] And just as some mothers are capable of child abuse, many fathers are capable of providing excellent care for young children. Yet in most cases Alice Rossi's 1978 statement still holds true: "The mother-infant relationship will continue to have greater emotional depth than the father-infant relationship because of the mother's physiological experience of pregnancy, birth and nursing."[37] She went on to note that while a society could try to override these biological propensities by training boys and men in infant care, it was not entirely clear how well such efforts might work out.

Women working in the household can nurture and care for older children at the same time that they produce additional children more easily than those employed in the market economy. This complementarity between childbearing and childrearing augments the scale of efficiency in the traditional sexual division of labor. Moreover, the biological differences between men and women have typically overlapped with and reinforced differences in the kinds of human capital investments they experience.[38] Thus, until recently, the efficiencies and comparative advantages of the traditional division of labor, which related largely to childrearing, resulted in special investments in education and training that would prepare women to assume the traditional homemaker's role and men to participate in the paid labor force. In 1960 relatively few college women were enrolled in prelaw, premed, or Ph.D.-oriented programs. Instead, they studied the liberal arts and sought to graduate with a B.A. Many also graduated with an "M.R.S."—the median age of marriage for women was 20.3 at that time.

All that has changed, however. Today more women than men are going to college, and they represent an increasing proportion of graduates from professional schools and Ph.D. programs. The biological propensities in support of the traditional sexual division of labor in childrearing have collided with the cultural forces of women's liberation. Women are investing substantially in increasing their human capital not for household productivity but for paid employment in the market economy. Accordingly, the median age for a first marriage has climbed to over twenty-five. Such changes have altered the calculations of efficiency and comparative advantage. When the income a female doctor or lawyer can earn pursuing a professional career outweighs the productive value of her household work, her time is worth more in the labor force than at home. For the lawyer's family members to get the most economic value out of the investment of their time, either they should outsource as much cleaning, cooking, and care work as possible or the husband should increase his participation in household work, particularly if he earns less than his wife. It might even make sense from a cost-benefit perspective for the husband to remain at home and take on all of the childrearing and household work—assuming that the intangible costs and benefits to the parents and children of this arrangement remained constant (a thought I shall revisit shortly).

As educational achievement advanced and employment opportunities expanded, many women expected to have a career, children, and a husband who would help clean, cook, and care for the kids—in sickness and in health and particularly in the middle of the night. This view emerged somewhat in response to the perception of shifting efficiencies and comparative advantages of engaging in household versus market activities. And it was reinforced by the idea that the traditional sexual division of labor was essentially a social construct that had very little to do with biological differences. From the 1960s to the mid-1980s the second-wave feminists, led by what Christina Hoff Sommers identifies as "gender" feminists, imagined that men could be convinced to renounce their socially constructed roles and step up to the plate—or, more accurately, the sink, the washing machine, and so on—to share equally in the traditionally female household and child-care duties.[39] Indeed, studies of the changing sexual division of labor suggest that some of this is happening—but perhaps not entirely as the gender feminists might have hoped.

There is persuasive evidence that despite all the changes in education and paid employment since the 1960s, women continue to assume the brunt of household and child-care responsibilities, resulting in what Arlie Hochschild dubs the "stalled revolution."[40] In countries where parental leave allows for fathers and mothers to share the time off from paid employment, for example, women consistently use more of the leave than men. And there is strong indication that when men earn less than their wives, they share even less in household work then those who earn more than their wives.[41] This behavior is explained as an effort to compensate for the damaged ego associated with failure to assume the normal (socially constructed) male identity as the primary breadwinner. Whether due to biological indispositions, inadequate socialization, insufficient ego, level of outside earnings, sluggish character, or some combination thereof, these findings suggest a degree of intractability in the roles men are willing to assume on the home front.

"Intractability" may be too strong a word, however, because the sexual division of labor has not remained constant over the decades. But precisely how much time and effort spouses invest in household and child-care duties is difficult to gauge. Even when examining nine-to-five employment, it is not easy to take an accurate reading of how people spend their time, except perhaps for a few occupations where time and activities are tightly framed by the job—for example, trolley drivers who stay on a track and lawyers who charge for their services by the minute. (A professor's work, by contrast, is never done—some say their best ideas have come while sleeping.) When it comes to family life, studies that derive estimates of unpaid household labor based on time-use diaries probably yield the most accurate information. Among recent studies using this method, two of the most thorough analyses reveal several prominent trends in the changing investments in employment, household work, and child-care activities since the mid-1960s.

Findings on the balance between paid and unpaid work from 1965 to 1999 show a changing pattern of behavior among men.[42] Although women did about 40 percent more unpaid work than men in 1999, the amount of time men devoted to housework and child care had more than doubled since 1965, rising from an average of 6.2 to 14.7 hours per week. However, 50 percent of men's housework activities involved what are typically considered masculine chores, such as maintenance and outdoor work, whereas only 21 percent of women's housework concentrated on these activities.[43] Most of the increase in men's unpaid work took place between 1976 and 1985, after which it slowed to a crawl. Women substantially reduced their housework from an average of 30.4 hours per week in 1965 to 16.8 hours in 1999; however, their average investments in child care showed almost no difference, going from 7.4 hours per week to 7 hours per week. The latter finding bears further comment since this average includes women with and without children and does not distinguish between employed and stay-at-home mothers.

The amount of time devoted to child care is an ambiguous subject that lends itself to varying interpretations. Is a mother playing soccer with her fifteen-year-old daughter engaged in child care (noted in the time diary under the child-care category of time spent on outdoor play), or is this just a leisure activity? What about the parents watching from the bleachers while their children play Little League baseball or soccer (and watching the teams play even when their children are not on the field)? Under the category of time spent talking to kids, does a mother talking to her son while preparing dinner qualify to the same extent as sitting at the table having a cup of coffee and talking to her child? Then there is the issue of whether all child-care activities are socially equivalent. Since 1965 there has been a significant increase in the amount of time spent driving preschool children to and from day care. How does spending five hours a week driving to and from day-care centers (which is identified as a child-care activity in time-diary codebooks) measure up against reading and playing with a child for that amount of time?[44] If a mother spends two hours a week volunteering in her son's first-grade classroom, does it count as child care? Finally, there is the question of how to count "stand-by" time—when, for example, a two-year-old is napping but might get up at any moment hungry, wet, or ready to play. Babysitters and child-care-center employees are paid to stand by while children nap.

The ambiguity surrounding child care is complicated by the fact that today caring for children is a sensitive topic, particularly for the majority of employed women with young children. Mothers do not want to feel that by altering their traditional roles they have in any way shortchanged their kids. Thus, reporting on the 2006 findings from a highly detailed and methodologically rigorous study of parental time devoted to child care, Ann Hulbert offers the soothing interpretation that the latest data do not support "the concern that kids have been shortchanged as women have flocked to the work force." As evidence, she explains that "the sociologist Suzanne M. Bianchi and her associates at the University of Maryland have noted that the average employed mother in 2000 recorded the same amount of primary child-care time (roughly 10 hours a week) as the average at-home mom did in 1975."[45] Indeed, most stories in the national press emphasize, as Robert Pear did in the *New York Times*, that "despite the surge of women into the work force, mothers are spending at least as much time with their children today as they did 40 years ago."[46] This widely cited finding is accurate as far as it goes—but it is not the entire story.

According to Bianchi and her colleagues, in 2000, employed mothers devoted as many hours to primary child care (that is, activities focused predominantly on children—such as reading to and dressing them) as nonemployed mothers did twenty-five years earlier (Table 1). But in both 1975 and 2000, the number of hours spent on primary child care by nonemployed mothers was more than 60 percent higher than that of employed mothers. If by children being "shortchanged" Hulbert is referring to the amount of time spent with their mothers in primary care, then it is true that children of working mothers today are not at a disadvantage compared to kids of nonemployed mothers twenty-five years ago. By the same token, compared to their peers today with stay-at-home mothers, those children are receiving significantly less primary care.

Table 1. Average Time (in Hours) Devoted to Child Care Weekly for Children under Eighteen Years of Age

	Employed mothers	Nonemployed mothers	Difference
1975			
Primary care	6.0	10.7	4.7
Secondary care	3.1	6.8	3.7
Total	9.1	17.5	8.4
2000			
Primary care	10.6	17.2	6.6
Secondary care	3.9	10.1	6.2
Total	14.5	27.3	12.8

Source: Suzanne Bianchi, John Robinson, and Melissa Milkie, *Changing Rhythms of American Family Life* (New York: Russell Sage Foundation, 2006), table 4.4.

The gap widens when the amount of time spent in secondary child care is considered.[47] Secondary care involves the periods of time during the day in which respondents were engaged in an activity such as shopping, cooking, and watching television while with their children. The researchers "assume that children and parents can benefit from the interaction that takes place when care is secondary, even though there may be great variability in the intensity of the interaction."[48] Secondary care might include, for example, folding the laundry while keeping a watchful eye on a child engaged in independent play. Day-care centers after all do not distinguish between primary and secondary care; keeping a watchful eye on children while they are engaged in independent play or during nap time is just part of the job. In 1975 nonemployed mothers spent more than twice as much time involved in secondary child care as employed mothers did, a difference that increased to almost three times as many hours in 2000.

Combining primary and secondary care, in 2000 stay-at-home mothers spent twice as much time with their children as employed mothers did.

But even these figures do not tell the entire story. According to the study, a stay-at-home mother in 2000 spent fewer than four hours a day on total child care—a figure that would probably baffle any stay-at-home mother with a two-year-old. When the amount of care is averaged for all children, from newborn babies through eighteen-year-olds, the results mask an important disparity between the daily effort required to care for children in the developmentally crucial years of preschool life and that required for school-aged children who are away from home most of the day—regardless of whether the mother is employed elsewhere. Thus, it is reasonable to imagine that the considerable difference between employed and nonemployed mothers in average time devoted to care of all children under eighteen years of age increases when the focus shifts just to preschoolers.

The findings on the changing sexual division of household labor are less ambiguous and socially charged than those on child care. What accounts for the increase in household labor among men and the decrease among women? Some of the shift is no doubt attributable to changes in certain characteristics of the male and female populations between 1965 and 1999, including age, education, employment, and marital and parental status. Obviously, more women were at home caring for larger families in 1965 than in 1999, which meant there was both more time available and greater demand for cooking, cleaning, and the like. Also in 1999 there were more single men living on their own and thus responsible for household maintenance than in 1965. The other major factor is changes in behavior—for example, men in 1999 spent less time on the couch drinking beer and watching football and more time working in the garden or the kitchen.[49]

The degree of behavioral change is estimated by comparing the number of hours spent on household work by men and women in 1965 with the number of hours spent in 1999 by men and women with matching characteristics. For example, the housework habits of a woman (or man) who was a college graduate, employed, and married with two children in 1965 are examined against those of a woman (or man) in 1999 living in the same circumstances. According to this analysis, behavioral modifications accounted for most of the increase in men's housework up through 1990. But after 1990, the small uptick in men's housework was essentially due to changing characteristics among men—specifically, more men were living alone and cleaning bachelor pads. The analysts interpret the declining magnitude of behavioral adjustments as a sign that the extent to which men and women can rearrange their lives to accommodate both paid and unpaid work has hit a ceiling.[50] Ultimately, there are only so many hours a day available for reallocation by people who are employed full-time.

These findings shed empirical light on the extent to which modification of the traditional division of labor benefits capitalism and, more broadly, on how organizing one's life according to rational calculation of costs and benefits shapes family choices. From the rational-choice perspective it comes as no surprise that as women invest more time and effort in developing human capital to boost their market value, they devote less time and effort to household productivity associated with the long-established sexual division of labor. Although men have taken up some of the slack, the average weekly hours spent on housework by men and women combined fell by more than 20 percent between 1965 and 1999. Much of the decline was in discretionary work, such as mopping floors, shampooing carpets, dusting furniture and ironing underwear, which simply no longer gets done or is done less frequently.[51] And some of the reduction represents time-saving products—wrinkle-free clothing, self-cleaning ovens, and automatic sprinklers. A substantial amount of household production, however, has been outsourced to the market. People now hire experts to organize their closets and arrange their daily schedules. Food from supermarkets as well as precooked meals are purchased online and delivered to the door—sometimes with a discount if the delivery is not prompt. People also eat out more often. In 2000, forty-one cents of every dollar Americans spent on food was consumed in restaurants, compared to twenty-nine cents in 1987.[52] As women's labor has shifted from the home to the market, the art of good housekeeping has apparently fallen on hard times.

The family serves not only as a haven that nurtures its members' physical and emotional lives but also as an economic unit that produces all sorts of goods and services. Educating the young, cleaning the house, preparing food, even changing lightbulbs are all services that contribute to the standard of living. The economic value of these services is their market price when produced by others—teachers, chefs, housecleaners, and electricians. "Even if you buy a chocolate bar," says Stein Ringen, "it takes a tiny bit of additional work to remove the wrapping before you can enjoy it. That's work. Make no mistake about it: some people pay servants to do it for them. The Prince of Wales is said to have his servant squeeze out tooth paste for him on to his tooth brush." Based on careful quantitative analysis, Ringen estimates that in 1986 half of the per-person value of the total output of goods and services in Britain came from economic activities in families—more than half if the family's nonpaid care work is included.[53] Gary Becker also concludes that nonpaid family work accounts for half or more of society's economic activity.[54]

These estimates of the immense amount of family production underscore the huge transfer of goods and services to the market economy spurred by the 20 percent decrease in unpaid housework. Not only did changes in the traditional division of labor open the door to capitalist activity in the household, but they also diminished the mutual exchange of services among kin for reasons of emotional attachment and social obligation. As new modes of production emerged, the process of creative destruction (which Schumpeter took as an essential fact of capitalism) struck an intangible, yet profound, blow to family life.

In determining whether the rational cost-benefit approach has influenced women's roles in the division of family labor, I would conclude that probably neither men nor women are entirely responsive to rational choice as economists measure it, because of norms and values as well as biological propensities. That being said, they have responded palpably to the changing costs and benefits of the traditional sexual division generated by women's increasing investment in human capital. The response has been mostly in the direction of women investing their labor in the market instead of the household, for a better return and a higher material standard of living.

Psychic Income of Motherhood

To the extent that women's decisions about developing and investing their human capital are influenced by rational calculations of costs and benefits that seek, as economists put it, to maximize "utility"—sometimes referred to as happiness or self-interest—why would they ever choose to have children? A ridiculous question, some would say. But consider for a moment that, as Schumpeter pointed out, children are no longer an economic asset. On the contrary, today raising a child through age seventeen costs a two-parent, middle-income family an average of $153,600—and the costs rarely stop there.[55] Parents whose children graduated from high school in 2006 are looking at an annual cost of $12,875 for tuition, fees, room, and board at a four-year public college ($30,816 at a private college), and those with infants can expect to pay $35,600 a year for a public university ($85,200 a year for private school) by the time their kids are ready for college.[56] Not only are children costly to raise, they are noisy in the process, cumbersome to transport, and magnets for germs. In addition, concern for a child's well-being makes its parents lifetime hostages to fate. In the critical cost-accounting of utilitarian values, the concrete sacrifices of parenthood weigh heavily against the transcendental joys, which are difficult to gauge, especially in comparison to, say, a carefree vacation spent skiing at Squaw Valley or relaxing on the beaches of Santa Monica. The mental attitude formed by this accounting reminds me of a woman I once saw driving a shiny red Mercedes sports car with a license-plate frame that read, "She who dies with the most toys wins." The Mercedes was stopped at a light next to a mother and two children in a Ford SUV with a prominent sticker that read, "Proud Parent of Two Wagner Ranch School Honor Students." Bumper stickers have become a sign not only of one's politics but of the way people score life.

Some even argue that children detract from intimate relationships between adults. According to Daniel Cere, a prominent strand of contemporary scholarship on courtship focuses on "close-relationship theory," which "draws attention to the vexing impact of children on adult close relationships."[57] Reviewing a body of courtship literature in which children are either ignored or are portrayed as stressful hazards to marriage, Cere cites an influential book that devotes two chapters to examining the obstacles to satisfactory relationships. The first chapter surveys a variety of problems, such as drug abuse and alcohol, that might undermine relationships; the second chapter is dedicated entirely to children.

Despite the risks and costs of childbearing, many would argue that most, if not all, women really want to have children because that's what they are made to do. Childbearing as a biological imperative conveniently avoids the cost-benefit issue by invoking the authority of Charles Darwin himself. Once it has been established that humans are programmed to propagate their genes (otherwise, we would not be here), then the rational approach to family choices helps explain the different investments parents might make in *raising* their children after they have arrived.

Although the biological imperative may have impelled procreation among the earliest members of our species, the biological imperative seems less vital today. As an explanation of women's behavior, it hardly accounts for the dramatic rise in the proportion of childlessness over the past few decades. The biological imperative, of course, may vary in degree, with some women feeling an overwhelming urge to procreate (the traditional mothers), some having relatively little interest in the process (those in the postmodern group), and many others somewhere in between (spanning the neotraditional and modern categories). The choices of those in-between women would be most sensitive to prevailing perceptions of the costs and benefits associated with childrearing, which bring us back to the question of how the decision to have children is framed within the rational-choice perspective.

Childrearing, as we normally understand it, essentially involves altruistic behavior. Taking a leaf from the pages of Adam Smith, Becker notes that while selfishness is assumed to prevail in market transactions, altruism dominates in family behavior. It is a matter not of biological imperative but of costs and benefits. Parents readily sacrifice for their children, depleting economic resources that might otherwise be put to their own material pleasures, because the well-being of their children increases the parents' stock of happiness. According to Becker it is naive to assume that altruists do not benefit from the transactions that seem to yield only monetary sacrifices. In reality, he explains, "altruists receive psychic income in place of money income."[58] Empirically, this proposition is difficult to disprove. When people weigh the costs and benefits of an action and then choose to behave in ways that lead to a measurable gain in, say, leisure time or money, they have exercised rational choice to maximize utility. If they choose to behave in ways that involve sacrifice and loss of measurable benefits, it can still be claimed that they are exercising rational choice but weighing the benefits on a scale of emotional returns, which are not as easy to calibrate as time or money. In a sense, psychic income is a deus ex machina that resolves the potential conflict between the rational-choice model and altruistic family behavior, which might otherwise appear irrational from a cost-benefit perspective.

This is not to say that psychic income, or the intangible personal and emotional benefits that it represents, is imaginary. People frequently engage in calculated behavior that they know will incur measurable costs and tangible sacrifices, and in the end they still feel that they have gained in the bargain. When Jerry Brown was governor of California in the late 1970s, he once advised the University of California professoriate not to complain about their salaries, since the accounting did not include all the psychic rewards they derived from their positions. Publicly most faculty complained that they could not pay the mortgage or dine at Chez Panisse with psychic income. Privately, some faculty probably agreed that the governor had a point—which might explain the behavior of those senior professors who qualify for retirement pensions equal to virtually 100 percent of their salaries, yet continue to remain at their posts.

Undoubtedly, one of the important reasons women have children is the psychic income it is expected to yield. In this regard Schumpeter was correct, if somewhat inarticulate, when he noted that a vital benefit of motherhood was its "contribution to physical and moral health—to normality as we might express it." He might also have included the contribution of motherhood to the fulfillment of emotional life. Children beget one of the few transcendental experiences in life outside of drugs and religion, both of which have their own costs—and, perhaps, music, which ends when the curtain falls. Jewish people have a word for the psychic income of motherhood—*nachous,* the joy parents get from their children. The traditional congratulatory mantra of Jewish grandmothers—"They should only bring you nachous"—conveys a heartfelt wish for the essential reward of motherhood, which is hoped for but not certain.

Unlike hard currency, psychic income is elusive; we never know which individuals will enjoy it, what source it will come from, and what its worth is on the market. Children as a source of psychic income for motherhood pose a unique case in that they embody two characteristics—uncertainty and permanence—which combine to form an exceptional risk. The uncertainty about how much joy and emotional satisfaction a child will bring resides, on one hand, in the unknown traits of the newborn and, on the other, in the yet-to-be-established response of the mother. After all of the modern prenatal medical tests are conducted, one of the greatest unspoken fears of mothers-to-be is that their child may be born with severe handicaps or may develop disabilities as they mature, which would raise the intensity of altruism to a level the mothers did not bargain for. That may be an extreme example, but there are all sorts of traits—levels of activity, physical appearance, sex, and personality—that might elicit more or less emotional satisfaction. And while mothers naturally love their children, the depth of their responses—even to perfectly healthy children—varies and cannot be fathomed ahead of time. Some mothers enjoy being around small children and interacting with them more than others. Some mothers who love their children dearly have a difficult time enjoying more than short periods of time with them. There are employed mothers who are soon anxious to return to their jobs and place their children in day care, and others who dread leaving their toddlers. On the subject of childrearing, Calvin Trillin explains that he and his wife, Alice, "agreed on a simple notion: your children are either the center of your life or they're not, and the rest is commentary."[59]

The level of uncertainty about the psychic income (we might call it joy or emotional satisfaction) to be gained from children is probably greater than with other sources of psychic income, such as employment in highly gratifying work. But even if the uncertainty were the same from all sources, the gamble associated with the benefits of children is compounded by the fact that children are permanent. In comparison to other sources of joy, the benefit derived from children cannot be entirely imagined until it is acquired, and by then there is no refund available. No other altruistic activity is quite as irreversible—priests can leave the church, social workers can decide to sell real estate, even Mother Teresa could have left the slums of Calcutta if she was so inclined. The probability of divorce in modern times lends an added dimension of uncertainty—not about consuming the benefits of children but about sharing the long-term costs.

Having children is a gamble in which the mother's stakes on happiness are high and the risks are evident, but both are difficult to calculate with precision. Who can imagine the long-term pleasures and pains that await, from the ceaseless midnight demands of the early years to the warm routines of the three-to-eleven golden years to the separation struggles of the pestering teenage years to the welcome respite from teenage menace during the empty-nest years, which are interrupted by the intrusiveness of the roommate years when the grown children return home for an indeterminate period? Parenthood is a bewildering journey full of surprises—some more agreeable than others.

According to pathbreaking research by Noble prize–winning psychologist Daniel Kahneman and his colleague Amos Tversky on what they called "prospect theory," people have psychological tendencies that distort efforts to make rational choices under conditions of uncertainty.[60] One such tendency, identified as the "certainty effect," is commonly expressed when we are faced with a choice between a course of action that will lead to a guaranteed gain and an alternative course that will lead to a larger gain that is only probable but that on average will yield the better return. Although people are likely to be more highly rewarded by selecting the probable outcome, most are firmly inclined to take the guaranteed benefit. Consider, for example, the choice between being given $400 or taking a chance on $700 by playing a game of roulette that is set up to let you win eight out of ten times. Preferring the certainty of the smaller gain, most people will take the cash and run. We tend to be averse to risk, at least when the probability of gain is high.[61] When we hear that the proverbial bird in the hand is worth two in the bush, we rarely question under what percentage of the bushes we will find the two birds.

How well the certainty effect applies to decision making in the broader context of lifestyle choices, where nothing is really certain, remains an open question. Laboratory findings that people tend to underweight the value of outcomes that are probable in favor of those that are guaranteed are at best suggestive when it comes to decision making about motherhood. What they suggest is that when weighing the probable gains in psychic income from motherhood against the human capital that they will almost definitely accrue by staying in school for a few more years or against the paycheck that assuredly will arrive each week by going to work, young women will tend to choose the more certain outcome (even when the utility of motherhood would be higher than the other options).

Women's decisions to have children, however, are rarely a choice of now or never (at least not until the terminus of their childbearing years). For most women it is usually a choice of now or later. Therefore, to the extent that the certainty effect applies in this context, it would tend to encourage the postponement of childbearing. But the more time spent accruing education and work experience, the higher the costs of childbearing in terms of foregone wages. Moreover, if a woman waits until she is in her thirties to have her first child, it may not be possible to have a second.[62] At the intersection between capitalism and motherhood, as noted in Chapter 1, there is a trade-off over time between the rising value of human capital, which increases the capacity for production in the market, and the declining efficacy of biological capital, which reduces the odds for reproduction in the family.

But something is missing from this assessment of human behavior. Do women really sit down with a pen and list all the costs and benefits of childbearing, assign probabilities, verify certainties, and then calculate the opportunity costs in comparison to alternative choices regarding work, education, or taking a year off to be a ski bum in Aspen? And if they did that, how would they attribute precise values to the immediate costs, benefits, and probabilities that come to bear on this irreversible lifestyle decision? The answer, I think, is that surely certain highly specific calculations are made: Can we afford to pay the current rent? Will we need to move to a larger house? But, more generally, some vague reckoning is taken in which the values attributed to far-reaching lifestyle costs and benefits of childbearing are informed by normative expectations about what awaits one on the paths to motherhood, education, employment, and professional life.

Although economic considerations bear on choices about motherhood and commitments to work and family life, these personal decisions involve more than a rational processing of empirical information about costs and benefits. In advancing a socioeconomic view of human behavior that incorporates the nonrational aspects of decision making, Amitai Etzioni argues "that the majority of choices involve little information processing or none at all, but that they draw largely or exclusively on affective involvements and normative commitments."[63]

Consider the choices facing Michelle and Becky. Michelle,

a stay-at-home mother, is feeling bored and unchallenged. She is thinking about returning to full-time employment. She expects that her family's income would increase, as would her skills and knowledge (what economists consider human capital). She could not tell us, though, exactly how much the family income would increase after discounting taxes, work expenses, child-care costs, and the economic value of her reduced household labor (and adding the value of the anticipated increase in her husband's household labor). She hopes her husband would be pleased with the decision and willing to cook meals several nights a week—but she is not sure. His job dealing with psychiatric patients takes its toll; he seems to rely on her steady emotional support and enjoys having her make coffee for him each morning. At the same time she recognizes that this decision would seriously reduce her daily relationships with all the other young mothers with whom she has been volunteering in her child's classroom, organizing swim meets, visiting at the playground and at their monthly book club meeting, and discussing the advantages of being able to supervise and socialize their children, while silently confirming the disservice of mothers whose children are raised five days a week by day-care workers—the very group Michelle would be joining.

Becky, a working mother, is feeling tense and pressed for time. She sees her kids growing up before her eyes, with little daily input from their mother. Her husband complains that she no longer makes his coffee in the morning and the house is a mess. She is thinking about returning home full-time. Becky knows that her family's income would decline—though, like Michelle, she could not say by exactly how much. At the same time she recognizes that her professional relationships (sometimes considered social capital) will decline as she loses touch with her friends and colleagues at the office, with whom she has been attending meetings, going to out-of-town conferences, trading advice on social and legal issues, and socializing at office parties. And she expects to miss the lively lunches at the local café during which her female colleagues debate the intellectual issues that animate everyday life in their firm, while silently confirming the utter, mind-numbing boredom of daily life for women at home (whom Becky would be joining) who spend their time cooking, cleaning, and changing diapers.

Michelle and Becky are facing hard decisions. The choices they contemplate violate their peer group's expectations and defy their hierarchy of values. But what if Michelle's decision was being made in 1965, shortly after her book club read Betty Friedan's *The Feminine Mystique* and Simone de Beauvoir's *The Second Sex?* And what if Becky's decision was being made sometime in the future, say 2013, when the opt-out revolution is in full swing?

In both cases economic considerations come to bear as well as affective involvements and changing social norms and values. Seen strictly from an economic perspective, notions of human behavior based on utility and rationality lead us to conclude that the benefits of motherhood are consistently undervalued by the prevalent sensibilities and habits of mind attuned to the opportunities in modern capitalist societies, and that this happens for two main reasons. First, the deep-seated emotional pleasures and transcendental rapture of child-rearing are not as tangible on the cost-accounting ledger as the material comforts and alluring amenities of a childfree lifestyle. Second, the indeterminate psychic income, those joys and emotional satisfactions, of motherhood is discounted by psychological preference for the certainty of alternative outcomes.

The economic perspective is useful in that it opens a partial window to the dynamics that influence women's lifestyle decisions; however, the view from this window excludes important social considerations that weigh on decisions about motherhood and family life. For a fuller picture, we must examine the values and expectations that have been most widely conveyed by those who speak publicly for women's place in modern society.

Chapter IV
Feminist Expectations: Who Suffers from the Problem That Has No Name?

The women's movement for equal opportunity in the 1960s spawned tremendous gains in educational achievement and labor-force participation. Not only has women's share of college enrollments increased (from 37 percent in 1960 to 57 percent in 2002), they work harder at their studies than men and walk off with a disproportionate share of honors (which may complicate life when the time comes for finding a mate with equivalent educational achievement).[1] Since the mid-1980s more bachelor's and master's degrees have been awarded annually to women than men. And women are increasingly going on to careers in high-status occupations, such as medicine, law, business, and higher education. These advances have been accompanied by a steady decline in women's participation in the productive and reproductive labors of motherhood, as reflected in the shrinking size of families, reduced hours of household work, and increased outsourcing of child care and other services previously performed by stay-at-home mothers. As women's labor has shifted from the home to the market, family life has been sold on work. How has this come about?

One reason often heard for the rise of two-earner families and the decline in family size is that nowadays it costs too much to raise two or more children on the average paycheck of a one-earner family. The high cost of living is real. Ask anyone in the San Francisco Bay Area, where the price of what used to be called a bungalow—with two bedrooms—starts at around half a million dollars. In 1970 I paid $25,000 for my first home, a wooden two-bedroom one-and-a-half bath bungalow in the Berkeley hills. Seven years later it sold for $100,000. Needless to say, a professor's salary did not increase by 400 percent in seven years. Today that bungalow would be advertised as a charming rustic house with a filtered view and go for more than $750,000.

Basic Necessities or Escalating Lifestyles?

When most of the working people I know in the San Francisco Bay Area talk about the need for two incomes to afford a home, they're making a fairly accurate calculation. (And even then, the two incomes have to be well above the national median.) But living in this area is a conscious lifestyle choice, even though for some the desire to live in a socially vibrant, picturesque, anything-goes community like San Francisco may be so strong that no other options are seriously entertained—the decision feels more like a preordained lifestyle verdict than a choice.

Still, it is a choice that many people forego. When faced with the costs and the implications for family life, they move to Oregon, Texas, or someplace else where the price of a San Francisco studio condominium buys a large family home. Between 1995 and 2000, more than 200,000 people migrated out of San Francisco, a large proportion of whom were families with young children.[2] A 2005 survey reported that 45 percent of families with children under age six expected to leave the city within the next three years.[3] Since 2001 the net outflow of people from California has increased fivefold in response to soaring house prices. Many are settling in less glamorous locales. The population transfer from California to Missouri, for example, more than tripled between 2001 and 2004. Melanie and Nathaniel Fischer and their three children were among the 2,200 California transplants to Missouri in 2004. They traded their home in California for a five-bedroom house that was nearly twice as large, and they purchased a twenty-one-foot boat with the money left over. "You have to give up things," Mrs. Fischer explained, "to get things." One of the things she got from the lower cost of living in Missouri was the opportunity to quit her job and stay home with her three children.[4]

Couples with young children who leave the California sun to purchase family homes elsewhere are not the norm, however, and they are probably not low income. What about poor people? Are two-earner households required for economic survival in low-income families with children? Is it necessary for both parents to work continuously during the early years of childrearing? Even among low-income families, much—if not most—of the requirement for a second income, which is attributed to economic necessity, is less a matter of obtaining essential goods and services than commonly recognized.

In the United States the basic point of reference for any discussion of low-income families is the poverty index formulated by the labor economist Mollie Orshansky in 1963. Orshansky's remarkably simple measure took the cost of the Department of Agriculture's Economy Food Plan for different household sizes and multiplied these figures by three, based on the fact that families spent, on average, about one-third of their income on food.[5] Since then, the poverty threshold has been adjusted slightly from year to year according to changes in the Consumer Price Index. In 2006, for example, the poverty line was $20,000 for a family of four composed of two adults and two children and $13,200 for a family of two. The Census Bureau estimated a national poverty rate of 12.6 percent in 2005.

Although the official measure of poverty is concrete, plausible, and convenient to use, many questions have been raised about how accurately it reflects the number of low-income people and their material well-being. Those who argue that the index overestimates the level of poverty point out that the calculation does not include other forms of income, such as the cash value of food stamps, housing assistance, Medicaid, energy assistance, school breakfast and lunch programs, the Earned Income Tax Credit, home equity (when converted to annuity), and income from cohabitants.[6] Others claim that the index underestimates the conditions of poverty because it overlooks additional factors that should be taken into account, such as child care and other costs of working, changing perceptions of basic necessities, geographical differences in costs of living, and a sense of relative deprivation that defies measurement by an absolute standard of adequacy. The technical debate on defining poverty includes many valid points by experts on all sides of the issue.[7] While the debate continues to refine the issues and challenge professional orthodoxy, the established index remains the basic reference for estimating (however roughly) the breadth and depth of material privation in the United States.

A glaring problem with the current measure from the layperson's perspective is that 46 percent of poor households own their own homes, which on average are three-bedroom structures with one-and-a-half baths, a porch or patio, and a garage—a picture that does not correspond with the popular conception of poverty. As for actual living space, the average number of square feet per person in poor households is considerably less than in nonpoor households; however, poor households in the United States averaged 10 percent more square feet per person than the average European household (from among the fifteen countries that were original members of the European Union). In 2001, the median value of houses owned by the poor was $86,000, which amounts to 70 percent of the median value of all homes in the United States.[8]

It should be pointed out that home ownership by households categorized as poor in the United States is highly concentrated among the low-income elderly, whose decisions regarding childrearing and patterns of labor-force participation were made decades ago. But even when we take into account the circumstances of the entire poverty population, poor households appear to have a degree of material consumption that defies efforts to explain the decline in childrearing and family size that has taken place since the 1970s as a result of economic necessity. For example, households living below the poverty line in 2001 enjoyed a level of material convenience similar to that of the general population in 1971 (Table 2). Yet the U.S. fertility rate in 1971 was 2.28, compared to 2.03 in 2001.

Although low-income households possess more conveniences of modern life than ever before, a 2006 survey conducted

Table 2. Comparison of Material Conveniences in the United States: Poor Households in 2001 vs. All Households in 1971

Percentage of households with	Poor households, 2001	All households, 1971
Washing machine	64.7	71.3
Clothes dryer	55.6	44.5
Dishwasher	33.9	18.8
Refrigerator	98.9	83.3
Freezer	28.6*	32.2
Stove	97.7*	87.0
Microwave	73.3	<1.0
Color television	97.3	43.3
VCR/DVD player	78.0	0
Personal computer	24.6	0
Telephone	76.7*	93.0
Air conditioner	75.6	31.8
One or more cars	72.8	79.5

Sources: W. Michael Cox and Richard Alm, "By Our Own Bootstraps: Economic Opportunity and the Dynamics of Income Distribution," *Federal Reserve Bank of Dallas Annual Report* (1995), 22; Robert Rector and Kirk Johnson, "Understanding Poverty in America," *Backgrounder*, January 5, 2004.

*Data for 1994

by the Pew Research Center found that over the last ten years many of these products, such as dishwashers, air conditioners, and cable television, had shifted in the public's perception from luxuries to necessities.[9] In maintaining that the average material condition of low-income people is better today than it was in 1970, my point here is not to exalt the life circumstances of the poor. Living on or near the poverty line today is, at best, a disagreeable state of affairs. And significant material discomforts are suffered by a relatively small percentage, but nevertheless large number, of people living in abject poverty—far below the established threshold. Still, it is clear that in modern times, "low income" is not synonymous with a lack of basic necessities that would entirely dissuade people from having children or require continuous employment by both parents for survival. Despite the many appliances and gadgets the public now considers impossible to live without, it is hard to argue that life was tougher in the 1970s, when proportionately more women had more children than today. Currently, even among the poorest of the poor—those people receiving assistance under the Temporary Assistance for Needy Families program—families have an average of two children.

Let us turn for a moment to the European Union countries, where the female labor-force participation rate is high and the average fertility rate is considerably lower than that of the United States, as are the poverty rates as defined by these countries (though these measures too must be taken with a grain of salt).[10] In 1942, looking beyond the struggles of World War II, English economist Lord Beveridge posed the great battles to come as the fight against want, disease, squalor, ignorance, and idleness.[11] Taking a measure of the European condition in 2006, Jens Alber concludes that these problems have been overcome. He summarizes the four new challenges facing Europe as children, care, careers, and college education.[12]

The low fertility rate in Europe is not explained by financial duress. Data on thirteen European Union countries show that the decline in motherhood and family life correlates with a rise in leisurely pursuits. Between 1987 and 1996 a proportional decline of 3 percent in the average fertility rate was accompanied by a proportional increase of more than 10 percent in the average amount of money spent on entertainment, recreation, and cultural activities.[13] As people had fewer children, discretionary spending on pleasurable interests increased.

However one interprets the data on the United States and Europe, they do not argue that either lower fertility rates or the increasing proportion of two-earner households are closely associated with the inability to otherwise afford the basic necessities. Assuming a family is not impoverished to start with, the choice to have a two-earner household with fewer than two children appears to be based on preferences for the immediate and tangible gratifications of material consumption over the distant and transcendental satisfactions of creating and nurturing a young life. But even this trade-off does not entirely capture the essential motivations behind the declining role of motherhood, since the actual value derived from a second earner in many families with children is not as large as it may seem, particularly during the early years of childrearing.

Although a second income may lift the heads of an impoverished family above the waterline, the added value of a second income in working- and middle-class families is often marginal, especially for those in jobs on the bottom half of the income ladder with a child or two of preschool age. There is considerable shrinkage in the real consumption value of the second income once the value of lost household production (discussed in Chapter 3) is taken into account, along with the costs of work-related expenses and increased taxes.[14]

The costs of child care vary widely depending on the age of the child and the quality of the care. High-quality care for preschoolers is expensive. There is no getting around the fact that caring for young children is a labor-intensive operation. It can benefit from economies of scale, but only within strict limits. One adult simply does not have enough eyes, arms, or physical stamina to provide eight hours of quality care for six two-to-three-year-olds. According to the experts, current standards for quality day care call for staff with at least two years of college, a background in early childhood development, and CPR training. The recommended ratio of staff to children for high quality care is around 1:4 for children up to three years old.[15] Imagine, then, a modest eight-child center in which two qualified caregivers were each paid $25,000 a year including benefits, and the combined costs of insurance, rent, utilities, equipment, and food amounted to another $30,000. Keep in mind that this is a bare-bones operation with no nurses, special cooks, or fancy quarters, and that it pays a salary of slightly more than ten dollars per hour (for adults with two years of college).[16] Simple arithmetic suggests that it would cost upward of $10,000 per child to run such a place. Most child care in the United States is less expensive than this—but parents get the quality of care they purchase, and children pay the price.

At $10,000 per child, the cost of day-care service comes to about 45 percent of the median earnings for all women who worked (both full- and part-time) in 2003 and 33 percent of the median earnings for those who worked full-time.[17] The amount of the paycheck left in hand is even further reduced by work-related expenses and taxes. A detailed analysis by the Organisation for Economic Co-operation and Development (OECD), established by the advanced industrialized countries, estimates that in the United States 63 percent of a second earner's salary from a full-time, low-wage job (paying 67 percent of the average production worker's earnings) is consumed by child-care expenses, taxes, and reduced benefits.[18] This percentage of reduction was similar to the combined average for twenty-eight advanced industrialized countries.

After subtracting child care, taxes, and work-related costs, what remains of a mother's income would not substantially enhance the material lifestyles of many two-earner families with young children in which the woman made less than the $22,000 median (or the $30,000 median for those working full-time year-round) in 2003. Moreover, when the outlays required to compensate for the reduced level of household production, the increased working hours, and the heightened stress of two-earner families are factored into the equation, it is hard to imagine that the second income lends much of a boost to the overall quality of family life. But this assessment applies mostly to workers at or below the median income. Certainly the additional income from the 3.5 percent of women who earned $75,000 or more in 2003 would increase their family's material comforts considerably beyond the small bump in consumption generated by a second income from young mothers with low-to-middle wages.

The decline in family size and the shift in women's labor from the household to the market between 1960 and 2000 was a sweeping social change that cannot be ascribed to the press of economic necessity. (This general assessment should not be taken as a denial that there are still many women in dire need, particularly single mothers, who must work.) Although the desire for increased material comforts may have pulled women away from the traditional role of motherhood, in many two-earner families with young children the net financial gain is slim and the quality of family life is diminished. For some women, however, the reverse is true. There are always winners and losers with any large-scale social change. And it is usually the winners, in this case an intellectual elite of well-paid professional women, who are among the strongest advocates of change. Between the 1960s and the mid-1990s, these women helped to create and reinforce new expectations about modern life, self-fulfillment, and the joys of work outside the home.

Feminism and the Apotheosis of Work

The normative expectation that women should participate in the labor force to the same extent as men emanates from an ideology of gender equality, which was widely expressed by the most influential voices in the feminist movement between the 1960s and the mid-1990s.[19] (Of course, there were other voices seeking to define modern feminism as well, just as there were other issues beyond the labor-force participation of women, including abortion and sexual violence, on the feminist agenda.) Toward the mid-1980s alternative views about caretaking, the value of women's work, and the reality of dependency in everyone's life were gaining expression, but the advocates of gender equality continued to capture the imagination and shape the core movement until recent years.[20] The timing here is important because normative expectations do not change overnight. By the dawn of the twenty-first century, feminist support for a more flexible approach to work and family life, sometimes referred to as care feminism or relational feminism, was on the rise. This strand of feminist discourse emphasizes the value of care work and the need for women to have meaningful opportunities to choose how much of their lives to invest in paid work and childrearing.[21] Supporting this position, Anne Alstott argues that "a pluralist approach should grant each caretaker equal resources and permit her to decide for herself which life to lead."[22]

Feminist discourse on paid work and childrearing is evolving, and which, if any, points of view will eventually dominate is an open question. At this time, however, normative expectations about employment for women (shared by many men as well) remain strongly influenced by the feminist views concerning gender equality that were promoted up through the mid-1990s. As Cynthia Fuchs Epstein observed, in the writings of the 1960s and 1970s, feminists of all political persuasions subscribed to a core ideology aimed at transforming gender in the family and the marketplace.[23] Louise Tilly and Joan Scott maintain in the introduction to their historical analysis of women, work, and family that much of the theorizing in the early 1970s emphasized paid employment as the solution to the oppression of domestic life. Although Tilly and Scott are not convinced of this view, they note that "the link between wages and liberation for women also seemed to be associated with the idea that self-determination was possible in the labor market but not in the family."[24] And Wendy Kaminer notes that even though the Women's Freedom Network in the 1990s was not part of the liberal wing of feminist thinking, it still represented "a traditional strain of feminism that has focused on expanding individual opportunity, in the belief that the sexes can and should compete as equals in the marketplace."[25]

Comparing attitudes toward gender roles in ten member countries of the OECD, survey data from the 1994 International Social Survey Program reveal that the United States had the fourth highest score on an ideology index of gender equality, just below Norway, Sweden, and Canada.[26] Gender equality in this context is less about equal treatment without discrimination than about equal results in terms of men's and women's roles in family life and their attainments in the workplace.[27] The push to neutralize gender distinctions is driven by the idea that traditional differences between men's and women's investments in work and family life derive more (some would argue essentially) from socialization than from biology. The feminists' dilemma, as Alan Carlson puts it, "is that this movement—like all modern ideological movements—is at war with human nature."[28] Gender feminists assert that all the traditional differences between behaviors of men and women in work and family life are socially constructed.[29] They claim that, in the absence of expectations cultivated by traditional patriarchal society, the particulars of a satisfying life would be entirely the same for men and women. But the traditional expectations will not wither of their own volition. Thus, gender feminists have actively sought to establish a new pattern of socialization for men and women that raises expectations for equal participation at all levels in the labor force and in every facet of domestic work and childrearing. To date, these efforts have been more influential in changing the socialization of women than of men, although men have increased their investment of labor in domestic and childrearing activities.

Normative expectations about motherhood and gender relations have been changing well beyond the U.S. borders, throughout the industrialized world. In the mid-1980s and early 1990s an OECD report proposed policies aimed at altering what its authors saw as the entirely social construction of gender. The objective of these proposals was to discourage role differentiation in regard to men's and women's investments of time and labor in paid employment, domestic duties, and leisure.[30] The expectation that women should participate in the paid labor force throughout their adult lives has perhaps taken the strongest hold in the Nordic countries. As Lane Kenworthy explains, the Nordic approach "promotes greater gender equality because it better facilitates mothers' employment in terms of both joining the labor workforce and limiting the interruption that results from the birth of a child."[31] Strictly speaking, the movement to limit a young mother's absence from the labor force is not a Nordic approach—it is found mainly in Denmark and Sweden. Finland and Norway, as we will see later, take a rather different attitude.

The view of childbirth as an interruption in labor-force participation that should be limited as much as possible has not yet gained complete acceptance in the United States. However, the ideology of gender feminists embraces a powerful expectation that women should be engaged in a lifetime of paid employment—just as men are. Barbara Bergmann, one of the founders of the International Association of Feminist Economists, opposes the idea of extending child-care tax credits to include parents who care for their preschool children at home, because benefits for home care would reinforce traditional roles. She thinks that women's status has benefited from the willingness of mothers of very young children to work outside the home. Supporting a normative attitude that childbirth should result in no more than a brief intermission from work, she maintains that "all women workers have better job opportunities when the custom is for most new mothers to return to work very soon after the birth of a child."[32]

Support for the norm of continuous labor-force participation by women, occasionally punctuated by brief periods necessary for reproduction, is consistent with the male model of labor-force participation: you hit the ground running upon leaving school and stay in the race until retirement. A number of career lines require an early start, and in the competitive marketplace most lines of work demand a concerted effort in order to reach the top rungs of professional and executive leadership. If women are to keep up with men, they have to start working early and stay at it. The emphasis on women's continuous attachment to paid employment makes good sense and is particularly helpful for those women with ambitions to have a run on the fast track to high-powered positions in society.[33]

Yet, at the same time that the male model of a lifetime devoted to paid employment supports the American dream of mobility and success, it overshadows and to some extent blocks out alternative paths that might be equally sensible for women who have other ambitions in life. The norm of continuous labor-force participation ignores the implications of increasing longevity in recent times as well as the fact that having children and staying at home to raise them is not necessarily a lifetime occupation. It imposes a static view of women's roles and the value of their work throughout the life cycle, based on the demands of the market and traditional male activities. From a dynamic perspective, the economic value of parental care and household management is substantial during the early years of childhood and declines as children enter school. A home-care commitment of five to ten years would leave most mothers with thirty years or more in which to participate in the paid labor force.

Bringing into question the norm of continuous labor-force participation reframes the issue of motherhood and employment as a question of how to divide parental labor throughout the family's life cycle rather than a choice between a one-earner or two-earner family. For those seeking to create a balance between motherhood and employment, the essential issue becomes whether to follow the male model of starting a lifetime pattern of work immediately after school, which involves the concurrent performance of childrearing duties and labor-force participation, or whether to initiate a sequential pattern in which they fully invest their efforts in childrearing and paid employment at different periods.

Obviously, certain career options may be closed to women who opt for the sequential pattern of childrearing and labor-force participation rather than the male model. Starting in one's mid-thirties would make it difficult to become a mathematician, media personality, physicist, doctor, fashion model, professional athlete, politician, or multinational CEO. Also, there is a higher probability that those who follow a sequential pattern of full-time motherhood and paid employment will not reach the pinnacles of occupational success. Few people attain such career heights in any case. Room at the top is quite limited—the vast majority of people spend their lives laboring in the middle grounds of their occupations. Posing the sequential pattern as an alternative approach in no way forecloses the option of the male model—a continuous line of employment remains open for those with their sights on the heights of professional achievement.

Moreover, the sequential pattern of moving from one type of work (unpaid caregiving) to another (paid employment) is compatible with emerging trends in employment that reveal a decline among people in the workforce who devote their entire career to a single line of work. In recent years many people have been changing course in midstream. A 2004 nationwide survey of more than six thousand working adults found that 58 percent of the respondents had changed their careers—most of them more than once.[34] In addition, an increasing proportion of women over thirty years of age are enrolling in educational programs, which prepare them to enter or reenter the labor force at that stage of life. The National Center for Education Statistics projects that by the year 2014, approximately 27 percent of all women in degree-granting institutions will be over thirty years of age, up from 17 percent in 1970.[35]

Nevertheless, the expectation for women to follow the male model of continuous employment is still firmly in place, as suggested by the critical response to reports of well-educated mothers opting out of the paid workforce (a movement that, if it gains momentum, could elevate the sequential pattern as a countervailing feminist alternative). This work-oriented norm has taken such a firm grip because it promises women more than just equal status with men at the corporate table and economic gain with which to enhance materialistic lifestyles. The attractions of a constant connection to the labor force are powerfully reinforced by the frequently (and almost universally) expressed presumption that paid work confers social and psychological benefits on women, along with disparaging assessments of unpaid household work. This perception of the personal rewards of employment has come about mainly because the vast majority of those who publicly talk, think, and write about questions of gender equality, motherhood, and work in modern society are people who talk, think, and write for a living. And they tend to associate with other people who, like themselves, do not have "real" jobs—professors, journalists, authors, artists, politicos, pundits, foundation program officers, think-tank scholars, and media personalities. (As one of them, I am qualified to speak with some authority on the subject.) They are not wealthy captains of industry but members of an occupational elite that is in some ways more privileged than the run-of-the-mill CEO and CFO.

Of course, people who get paid to build knowledge, inform the public, and shape social policies work for their wages, and they often work hard at what they do. When I say that they do not have "real" jobs, I am referring to the fact that the kind of work they perform provides a degree of physical and temporal autonomy unknown in the typical work week of nine-to-five employment. Not only do such people enjoy an extraordinary level of discretion in deciding when and where their work is performed, but much of the time there is also considerable latitude regarding *what* they actually do—what they write, talk, and think about. Freedom to manage the when, where, and what of their labor increases the likelihood that it will be experienced as meaningful and enjoyable rather than oppressive.[36]

Among the professoriate, for example, most of my tenured colleagues in the social sciences and humanities at the University of California, Berkeley, are required to spend four to five hours a week, thirty weeks a year, teaching in a classroom. That is, their temporal and physical autonomy is limited by employment for about 120 to 150 hours a year. When faculty speak of "office hours," they mean the two or three hours a week spent waiting in their office for students to come by in search of advice (often the loneliest time in a professor's schedule). Such a schedule contrasts sharply with the standard nine-to-five, five-days-a-week schedule. According to Paul Graham, the most demoralizing aspect of the traditional office job is that you're supposed to be there at certain times: "The basic idea behind office hours is if you can't make people work, you can at least prevent them from having fun."[37]

Industrial production is no longer organized on the classic time and motion studies of Frederick Taylor, well known as the "father of scientific management." Yet, as Daniel Bell explains, "time rules the work economy, its very rhythms and motions."[38] In 2002 the average U.S. worker put in 1,815 hours on the job. For most workers, this time was spent at a particular place—office, shop, desk, factory—for prescribed hours performing designated tasks.[39] In academia, even the physical location of the work is flexible, and sometimes shifts from assigned classrooms to the professor's home or the local coffeehouse (if the class is small enough). Academic freedom also assures instructors substantive license to select the material they teach under a particular course heading. Preparation for classroom teaching is time consuming, but once a lecture is fine-tuned it often endures, since the knowledge conveyed in many subjects—the history of ancient Greece, experimental research design, introductory French—does not change dramatically from year to year.

In addition to teaching students in the classroom, faculty meet with and advise students, serve on academic committees, attend professional conferences, perform community service, and conduct independent research (which especially involves a major commitment of time and effort). With all these activities, many faculty work fifty hours a week during the thirty weeks of classroom teaching. Yet most of this work is of a self-directed, voluntary nature, marked by a high degree of physical and temporal autonomy and substantive license—as anyone on campus who has tried to organize a faculty meeting on a Friday can attest.[40] University teaching is by and large divorced from the normal discipline of everyday life in the marketplace. It bears only the faintest resemblance to most work in the real world.[41]

Moreover, some of the professional duties are arguably rather pleasant. Learned gatherings of academic associations are rarely held in Topeka, Kansas. Traveling instead to places like New York City, San Francisco, Paris, and Geneva, professors gather to present their latest findings, engage in lively intellectual discourse, and exchange gossip with old friends and academic colleagues from around the world, followed by a grand banquet in the evening—and they get paid for doing it (not royally, but well enough for the exertion).[42] Joining those whose views on social matters are taken seriously by the public, tenured professors are part of a privileged class of columnists, media commentators, think-tank pundits, and others that experiences the enjoyment of paid employment.

Temporal autonomy was not always reserved for the occupational elite. In the nineteenth century, cigar makers in Milwaukee went on strike to defend their right to leave the shop at any time without their supervisors' permission. This was not atypical. "During much of the 19th century," Tom Lutz observes, "there were more strikes over issues of time-control than there were about pay or working hours." About his own job, Lutz admits that "we academics do have something few others possess in this postindustrial world: control over our time," which surveys reveal as the most common factor in job satisfaction.[43]

But the joys of work are not evenly distributed. Tolstoy may have had it right that happy families resemble one another while unhappy families are all miserable in their own fashion. Whether one is happy or unhappy at home, however, there is considerably less variance in the demands of unpaid family work than in the demands of labor-force participation. Unpaid family work may be portrayed as shaping unformed personalities, nurturing relatives, and managing the household—or, in more pedestrian terms, caring, cooking, and cleaning. However it is presented, the scope of activities is relatively narrow in comparison to jobs in the paid labor force, which include, of course, caring, cooking, and cleaning. To say that there is less variance within home-centered work is not to say that it is less formidable or strenuous than paid employment, but that the scope of roles in paid employment is more diverse—ranging from, say, mining coal in the depths of the earth to flying airplanes at thirty thousand feet, or from sitting on a stool in a factory to holding a seat on a board of directors. The world of paid work encompasses a vast array of activities, from those that are low status, boring, physically demanding, poorly rewarded, and dangerous to those that are high status, exciting, physically easy, well rewarded, and safe—with the latter being in relatively short supply.

The privileged few with high-status, stimulating, and well-rewarded jobs tend to experience the social and psychological advantages of work, which they then broadly attribute to labor-force participation. They have the kind of jobs in which they think "doing lunch" is work. (Foundation officers, for example, know that upon accepting the post they will never again lunch alone or tell a joke that is not heartily appreciated.) For most workers, however, lunch is a one-hour break from labor to refuel their bodies for the next shift—or a midday meal they have to forfeit in order to run household errands.

To date, the prevailing norms for working mothers have been shaped by an influential core of the occupational elite who publicize the presumed universal social and psychological rewards of paid employment (which they themselves do experience), while ignoring the social and psychological benefits of unpaid caring and household work. Indeed, when unpaid labor is addressed, caregiving and household management are often depicted as servile, tedious, mind-numbing work of limited worth.[44] One might say it started in the mid-1960s, when Betty Friedan identified what she experienced as the oppressive drudgery of household work—"the problem that has no name."[45] Friedan graduated in the 1940s from Smith College, one of the elite Seven Sisters women's colleges of that period. By her own account, Friedan's marital life was a wretched affair, and there were accusations of domestic violence on both sides. As Dan Seligman points out, the problem that had no name may have been rooted to some extent in the tribulations of an unhappy marriage. He contends that *The Feminine Mystique* described a world "populated more or less exclusively by upscale college-educated women raising families in comfortable suburban homes in the 1950's."[46] The late Elizabeth Fox-Genovese agreed that in many respects feminism can be seen as an account of the lives of young, white, well-educated, and well-to-do women—a slice of the population for whom work offered not only additional income but also the promise of personal fulfillment.[47] Still, with three million copies of *The Feminine Mystique* sold in the United States, Friedan's gloomy depiction of domestic life must have resonated among many women in those circumstances.

Long before Friedan's discourse on the powerlessness and oppression of motherhood and domestic life, George Bernard Shaw offered an entirely different scenario. In his 1928 handbook entitled *The Intelligent Woman's Guide to Socialism and Capitalism,* Shaw wrote, "The bearing and rearing of children, including domestic house-keeping, is a woman's natural monopoly. As such, being as it is the most vital of all functions of mankind, it gives women a power and importance that they can attain to in no other profession, and that man cannot attain to at all. In so far as it is slavery, it is slavery to Nature and not to Man; indeed it is the means by which women enslave men."[48]

But it is Freidan's image of motherhood and domestic life that continues to exert influence. Writing in the early 1990s, Suzanne Gordon found that the low regard in which domestic activities are held creates an awkward dilemma: "Feminists cannot simultaneously applaud men who share caregiving in the home and helping professions and look down on women who freely choose to work in the home as mothers or who become nurses, teachers, child care providers, or social workers." She asks, "If work in the family wraps one in a haze of domesticity and enrolls one in a cult of domesticity that blunts all talents, why would any man volunteer for this social lobotomy?"[49]

The core group of gender feminists that framed this

negative image from the 1960s to the 1990s may have shrunk, but the view of household labor as an oppressive, boring grind continues to inform much of the public discourse. Indeed, among many elite professionals, it has become an uncontested fact of modern life.[50] Consider the following statement comparing paid employment and household work: "Paid work outside the home is necessary for the income it provides to purchase food, shelter, health care, and other goods and services on which individuals and families rely. Paid work also provides people with a sense of purpose and satisfaction, although it can produce stress. Unpaid work within the home—cooking, cleaning, shopping, home maintenance, and caring for children—is also necessary for the health and well-being of individuals and families. As with paid work, unpaid work provides satisfaction and fulfillment, *but much of this work is mundane and tedious*" (emphasis added).[51] The choice of words here is telling. After three lines that seem to offer a balanced view of paid and unpaid work, the statement concludes with a gratuitous reminder of the tedious and mundane existence of stay-at-home mothers. It is noted that paid work can produce stress, which seems a mild caution in contrast to the strong emphasis on the tedium of household work, which is not even demanding enough to be stressful. This quote is not taken from a 1970s publication of radical feminist persuasions. It comes from the introduction to a well-designed academic study of men, women, and work that was conducted by established scholars and published in 2004 by the Russell Sage Foundation—one of the oldest, most revered foundations supporting the study of social issues in the United States.

I can imagine readers asking, "Really, *isn't* much of cooking, cleaning, shopping, home maintenance, and caring for children tedious and mundane?" My response to that is, "In comparison to what?" Linda Hirshman claims that "the family—with its repetitious, socially invisible, physical tasks—is a necessary part of life, but allows fewer opportunities for full human flourishing than public spheres like the market or the government."[52] Many people would no doubt find unpaid household chores less interesting than Professor Hirshman's job or the paid work of the professors who wrote the Russell Sage Foundation report (or, probably, the work of many people who are reading this book and consider it part of their job). But walking up and down the supermarket aisle selecting food for a family dinner is a job that has more variety and autonomy than the paid work being done by the supermarket employees who stack the same shelves with the same food day after day, and those who stand in a narrow corner at the checkout counter all day tallying up the costs of purchases, and the workers next to them who pack the purchases into paper or plastic bags. That space in the market is a bit cramped for human flourishing. Is caring for one's child—changing the diapers as well as experiencing the joy and excitement that comes with the first smile, step, utterance—a more wearisome job than that of the paid worker doing the same thing for four or five children who are not their own? Does standing behind a counter all day, sitting in an assembly line, driving a bus, or cleaning offices at night allow more opportunities for human flourishing than nurturing children and managing a home?

Not everyone gives the same answer. When Meghan Cox Gurdon's second child was born she left an exciting job as a foreign correspondent to be a full-time wife and stay-at-home mother. The initial adjustment to spending all day with small people who clamored to be fed and showed no interest in foreign affairs took some work. She had to cope with a sense of diminished status, particularly when meeting up with former colleagues who wanted to know, "What do you *do* all day?" What she did all day—ferry kids around, plan playdates, load up on groceries, amuse and educate children, feed the family, keep everyone clean, and volunteer for schools—was outwardly unremarkable. She found, however, that "inwardly you feel you are the heart of your family. . . . Indeed, the dark secret of housewifery—the thing none of us knew until we gave up our paid jobs—is that it's fun. And it's deeply gratifying. Everyone gets frazzled occasionally, but one has the opportunity with this kind of life to escape the bruising rhythms of the larger world. We don't spend our time under fluorescent lights. We never have to face office politics. We don't receive paychecks, either, but we do have the luxury of time."[53]

The Joy of Work?

The assumption that women experience unpaid housework and child care more negatively than paid work bears critical examination. For many (if not most) women, empirical evidence suggests that this is not the case. In developing the Day Reconstruction Method, a sophisticated approach to assessing how people feel during their daily activities, Daniel Kahneman and his colleagues surveyed 909 employed women on how they had felt during sixteen different activities and interactions with eight different partners on the previous day, and analyzed their responses. Overall, respondents reported a much higher degree of positive affect than negative affect on all activities and interactions. In comparing specific experiences, however, the data showed that on average the employed women expressed a higher degree of enjoyment for shopping, preparing food, taking care of their children, and doing housework than for working at their jobs—an activity that was ranked at the next-to-lowest level of enjoyment, just above commuting to work. Similarly, they experienced a higher level of negative affect while at work than while cooking, cleaning, shopping, and caring for their children. When it came to interactions with different partners, the women ranked interactions with their children as more enjoyable than those with clients/customers, co-workers, and bosses.[54]

Of course, one study—even one by a highly distinguished team of researchers—does not dispose of the "problem that has no name," in part because this is a study of employed women, which does not tell us how stay-at-home mothers experience their daily activities. Employed women might find cooking, shopping, cleaning, and caring more enjoyable because they usually spend less time on these activities than stay-at-home mothers do. It would be impossible, however, to compare the level of enjoyment experienced by stay-at-home mothers during various activities throughout a particular day to the level of enjoyment experienced during paid employment that same day. As Kahneman and his colleagues indicate, other studies based on global ratings showed that while interactions with children topped the list of enjoyable activities, shopping and housecleaning were rated below working at one's job. They note, however, that these ratings were less rigorous and more prone to discourage socially inappropriate responses than the assessments of specific episodes in their own study. Moreover, while these types of studies provide a highly systematic account of how people experience specific episodes of activity throughout a day, they beg the question of whether discrete affective responses to daily activities actually add up to a personal sense of happiness and fulfillment. (Is a state of happiness more than the sum of temporary pleasures?) A national survey of 2,020 adults in 2007 reports that 85 percent of parents rated relationships with their young children as the aspect of their lives most important to their personal happiness and fulfillment—far above their jobs or careers.[55]

Although the empirical research is inconclusive, however one interprets the data they do not comport with the pervasive feminist view of paid employment as an everyday source of enjoyment for women and unpaid family work as a source of tedium. The voices of those in the privileged occupations speak most often of their own felicitous work experiences and their perceptions of the gratification that men in their circles reap from work. It is an authentic assessment based on a self-referential slice of reality, which fails to reflect the working lives of a large proportion of women and men in jobs marked by stress, tedium, and emotional exhaustion.

Thirty years ago researchers in applied psychology identified the problem of work-related burnout.[56] Burnout has since become a burgeoning field of study, with competing empirical definitions that place varying emphases on emotional exhaustion, depersonalization, and lack of personal accomplishment (according to the widely used Maslach Burnout Inventory); fatigue (from the Copenhagen Burnout Inventory); and exhaustion and disengagement (from the Oldenburg Burnout Inventory).[57] In all accounts, burnout bears a curious resemblance to Friedan's problem that has no name.

Women seeking to escape the oppressive drudgery of unpaid work for the pleasures of employment supposedly enjoyed by men might ask why the average male worker hastens to begin retirement as quickly as possible. The evidence here is quite firm. During the past ten to fifteen years many of the industrialized countries have made policies and plans to raise the normal age of retirement either directly or indirectly by increasing the required period of contributions. Meanwhile, voting with their feet, an increasing proportion of men in the advanced industrialized nations have been exiting employment well before the standard age of retirement. In nine major OECD countries, the average percentage of men ages fifty-five to fifty-nine who were employed declined from 72.2 percent in 1987 to 69.2 percent in 1999—meaning that by 1999 almost one man in three was retired by his mid-to-late fifties. For men ages sixty to sixty-four, the percentage declined more steeply from 45.1 percent in 1987 to 40.6 percent in 1999. In 1999, on average 50 percent of the men in these countries withdrew from the labor force at 62.3 years of age or younger (the age for women was 61.1) and 25 percent of the men withdrew from the labor force at 58 years of age or younger (57.4 for women). Since 1987, the overall trend has moved clearly toward early retirement, and despite a slight tick upward in recent years, the average age of retirement still remains well below sixty-five.[58]

Some suggest that this trend has been spurred by generous pension benefits that create incentives for early retirement—either inadvertently or by design. Although pension incentives may be a factor contributing to early retirement, the attitudes expressed in international surveys convey sober evidence about the presumed benefits of work. Findings from the International Social Survey Program's 1997 Work Orientation Study, which included more than ten thousand respondents in eight OECD countries, suggest that given the choice, the majority of those in retirement would not have preferred to remain employed.

A close look at the data shows that responses vary somewhat depending on how the survey questions were posed. When asked, "Suppose you could change the way you spend your time," an eight-country average of only 8.8 percent of retired respondents answered that they "wanted to spend more time in a paid job." Among two other groups outside of the labor force, an eight-country average of 28.7 percent of those currently keeping house said they wanted to spend more time in a paid job, and surprisingly an average of only 55.8 percent of unemployed workers indicated wanting to spend more time in a paid job. Similarly, among those with part-time jobs, only 28 percent wanted to spend more time working.

When the question was posed in a slightly different form—"Suppose you could decide on your work situation at present, which would you choose?"—an eight-country average of 37.5 percent of retired respondents indicated that they would choose a full-time job. What accounts for the seeming contradiction between only 8.8 percent of retirees wanting to spend more time in a paid job and 37.5 percent of retirees who would choose a full-time job if they could decide on their work situation? One explanation is that the latter respondents might have interpreted being able to decide on their work situation as a license to select the most satisfying jobs they could imagine—desirable positions of authority, status, temporal autonomy, and free travel to conferences—which they would be pleased to enter on a full-time basis. The retirees' responses to a third question lends a certain degree of credibility to this explanation. When asked how easy or difficult they thought it would be to find "an acceptable job" if they were looking actively, an eight-country average of only 14 percent felt an acceptable job would be easy to find, which is much closer to the 8.8 percent who indicated that they would want to spend more time in a paid job.[59]

These findings gain further support from a 2005 study of 6,244 employed men and women in ten European countries. Although there was some variation among the countries, overall a high proportion of the respondents indicated their intention to retire early—more than 50 percent in half of the countries. Moreover, when the respondents were divided into three groups according to the quality of their jobs, an unambiguous pattern emerged across the ten countries, with employees in the lower-quality jobs consistently expressing the intention to retire early more often than those in less-stressful jobs.[60] In the United States a 1999 *Newsweek* poll of 492 workers found that 39 percent of the respondents hoped to retire before their fifty-first birthday, if they could afford it, and 26 percent said they expected to retire before age sixty.[61]

Many workers are retiring from the labor force as quickly as they can, most people who choose household work do not seem anxious to trade for more time in paid jobs, and even many unemployed people express little desire to spend more time in paid jobs. These findings suggest the need for a frank corrective in the prevailing discourse on work and family life led by academics and other members of the occupational elite. It is not entirely uncommon for academics to advance revelations about their personal circumstances as universal truths. A classic example is Sigmund Freud's formulation of the Oedipus complex, which drew heavily from his childhood feelings of love for his mother and jealousy of his father. Writing to his friend Wilhelm Fliess in 1897, Freud made it clear that after reflecting on this personal experience he now considered such feelings "a universal event in early childhood."[62]

When members of the occupational elite write and talk about the joys and personal fulfillments of work, they should admit that what they really mean is *their* work. They are not referring to the work of those in their own institutions who stay chained to desks all day, clean floors, or empty wastepaper baskets—the mostly female clerical and cleaning staff. They are not talking about the subway, taxi, and bus drivers who take them to work, the cooks and waiters who make it possible for them to do lunch, or the clerks serving behind the counters in the stores they pass on the way to work. And they certainly are not recalling Marx's indictment that "factory work exhausts the nervous system to the uttermost, it does away with the many-sided play of muscles, and confiscates every atom of freedom, both in bodily and intellectual activity."[63] But one need not invoke Marxist rhetoric to recognize that while some jobs are interesting and fulfilling, the majority simply are not, and are unlikely to become so.

Of course, work is necessary. According to Freud, "No other technique for the conduct of life attaches the individual so firmly to reality as laying emphasis on work." But here he was talking about professional work, and abilities and gifts accessible to only a few people. "And even to the few who do possess them," he said, "this method cannot give complete protection from suffering."[64] The idea of attaining happiness through work, while true for a fortunate few, makes a virtue of necessity for the many.

The Myth of Independence

If paid employment does not confer happiness on many mothers, or at best offers no more happiness than they might experience investing their labor at home with their children, it is at least supposed to make them independent. Feminist ideology conveys the popular expectation that liberated women achieve independence through work in the marketplace. Independence is a highly valued attribute. But what exactly does it mean in the context of family relations? Mothers and fathers want their children to grow up to be independent in the sense that they should be able to think for themselves, act autonomously, and eventually move out of the house, set up their own home, and take care of themselves. But do mothers and fathers want the same kind of independence in relation to each other? They may want their partners to be people who think for themselves and are able to act autonomously, but do they want partners who are preparing to eventually move out of the house, set up their own home, and take care of themselves?

Family life has been displaced by work because feminist expectations have framed the idea of a liberated, independent woman as one who is not economically dependent on her spouse. A psychological distinction can be made, however, between the capacity to manage what comes our way in life, which I think of as self-sufficiency, and the desire to be economically independent of one's partner. Self-sufficiency involves the ability to take care of oneself, not in the narrow sense of economic self-support but in dealing with the contingencies of daily existence. Self-sufficiency is a human quality that speaks to a much broader and deeper set of competencies than independence, which conveys merely an autonomous state of being—or not being controlled by others. A personal sense of self-sufficiency frees one psychologically from concerns about being controlled by others. In contrast to independence, which emphasizes freedom from control, self-sufficiency is more amenable to interdependent relationships, in which family members may feel confident dividing social powers and responsibilities.

Going to work confers independence in a particular sense for married mothers: their financial reliance on their husbands is diminished. This is liberating to the extent that they are married to men who want to or try to rule the roost through control of the purse strings. But even in these homes the economic independence gained through employment is in a larger sense paradoxical. At the same time that the employed wife's paycheck liberates her from financial dependence within the family, it heightens her vulnerability to interpersonal constraints imposed by strangers—bosses, customers, and clients—and to the vagaries of the marketplace. She may encounter the same subjugation experienced by the typical "independent" male breadwinner, including bullying, which has become so widespread in the workplace that Robert Sutton's book on building a civilized workplace, *The No Asshole Rule,* jumped to number ten in the Amazon.com sales ranking within a month of publication (the unconventional title might have lent a boost).[65]

For most men and women working for a wage, the independence that comes with a paycheck is accompanied by obedience to the daily authority of supervisors, submission to the schedule and discipline of the work environment, deference to customers, and susceptibility to the mounting insecurities of modern-day employment. Indeed, as the person who cares for his children, prepares his meals, and bestows physical warmth and affection, the dependent mother has much greater power in her relationship with her husband, on whom she relies for economic support, than the average independent mother has in her relationships with her boss and customers, on whom she relies for her paycheck. There are exceptions, of course, as already noted. Those at the top of the pyramid in business, politics, arts, and academic and professional life—the occupational elite who trumpet the empowerment of work—experience a degree of independence; those employed lower down the scale experience supervision, repetition, daily regimentation, and exposure to consumer demands.

In two-earner families, the spouses' economic independence from one another is acquired at the cost of the family's increased dependence on the market economy to meet many of the needs previously satisfied by the family members for reasons of mutual obligation and personal affection. When mothers of young children join the paid labor force, the caring, nurturing, and home management functions of family life are typically outsourced to day-care centers, cleaning services, and fast-food chains and local restaurants. As the work of unpaid household labor is transformed to paid employment, scenarios such as the following become increasingly common: Parents with two young children rise at six in the morning; prepare breakfast; wash, feed, and clothe the kids; and drop them off at day care, which might be subsidized by the state as much as $10,000 to $12,000 per child. The mother then heads off to her job—perhaps at another day-care center, where she is employed to look after other peoples' children. One could draw a similar scenario involving a woman who works in a nursing home for the elderly instead of staying home to care for her disabled mother. Both cases involve a shift from voluntarily caring for children and elderly kin out of a sense of devotion and commitment to performing caring services for strangers for pay.

As mothers have entered the labor force, families have become more dependent on the state and market to supply the care work once performed for free—and throughout the industrialized world most of this paid care work is still carried out by women. This is the case especially in the Scandinavian countries, despite their reputation for promoting gender equality and liberating women from the confines of domesticity. In Sweden, 75 percent of the jobs created from 1970 to 1990 provided social welfare services in the public sector; almost all these jobs were filled by women.[66] In Denmark, 64 percent of women's contributions to labor-force growth between 1960 and 1981 took place in day-care centers, nursing homes, and schools. Similarly, in Norway, women staff the vast majority of civil-service jobs that carry out functions once performed privately, within the household. Thus, as Alan Wolfe makes clear, "The distribution of sex roles has not greatly changed in Scandinavia (gender-defined work has probably been more thoroughly transformed in the United States), but their character has changed greatly: they have become 'nationalized,' in the sense that the Scandinavian welfare states organize through taxation and public services activities for all of society that were once undertaken more intimately and privately."[67] The taxes that support these services come in large part from the paychecks of families, including the very wives and mothers who perform the work. For a large proportion of women, the sense of independence gained from paid employment comes with all sorts of strings attached.

Although feminist expectations about the social benefits of work do resonate with the ambitions and experiences of some women, they ignore the interests of many women, particularly those in the middle and working classes. Even among the upper tier of professional elites, some women with young children appear to be having second thoughts about the levels of personal enjoyment and independence that are actually derived from paid employment. If I maintain that many mothers have been oversold on the economic and social benefits of continuous labor-force participation, it is not to argue for a return to the traditional view that women belong barefoot, pregnant, and in the kitchen. Rather, it is to suggest that public discourse on work-family choices give voice to a balanced perspective, one that lends due consideration to women's diverse interests and values and to the full range of options for managing work and family responsibilities over the course of an eighty-five-year lifespan.

The idea of a more balanced assessment of work-family choices has not been received with universal enthusiasm. When Betty Friedan suggested that women should have the choice to stay home and raise kids if they wished, Simone de Beauvoir responded, "We don't believe that any woman should have this choice." She believed that "no woman should be authorized to stay home to raise her children . . . because if there is such a choice too many women will make that one."[68] That was thirty years ago, but those sentiments continue to resonate among some high-profile feminists. In 2006, for example, Linda Hirshman argued that because housekeeping and childrearing offer fewer opportunities for full human flourishing than working for business or government, assigning family work to women is unjust. Moreover, she writes, "women assigning it to themselves is equally unjust. To paraphrase, as Mark Twain said, 'A man who chooses not to read is just as ignorant as a man who cannot read.'" In a not-too-deft shuffle, Hirshman moves from declaring a woman's choice to invest her labor in family life "unjust" to equating it with "ignorance."

What young women need, according to Hirshman, is not choice, but guidance from their elders on how to gain access to money, power, and honor. To this end she offers a recipe for independence. First, young women should prepare for work by studying liberal arts less, instead taking courses more likely to lead to good jobs and working after graduation with an eye to the future. Second, they should treat work seriously. The best way to do that, she suggests, is to find the money. Third, to ensure that their spouse will do an equal share of housework, they should either marry down—younger, poorer men—or marry much older, well-established men who have enough money to pay for household help. Finally, they should not have more than one child.[69]

Hirshman's advice was delivered not on an obscure feminist weblog or in an alternative newsletter but in the *American Prospect,* a well-circulated and highly regarded journal of liberal persuasion, thus signifying that in some quarters de Beauvoir's resistance to choice still animates an influential strain of feminist thinking. At the same time, among the current generation of well-educated women there are signs of change in the rise of care feminism and hints of an opt-out revolution, which challenge prevailing assumptions and kindle public discourse about how much to invest in motherhood and in the paid labor force—and about how individual women may value the intrinsic worth of these endeavors. This fresh outlook not only examines the impact of earlier feminist expectations about work but also questions the extent to which these expectations are reinforced by the role of the state in advancing family-friendly policies.

Chapter V

How Family Friendly Are Family-Friendly Policies?

The shift of women's labor from unpaid care and household management to paid employment has been advanced by an array of social policies aimed at reducing the friction between work and family life. These "family-friendly" policies typically include a package of benefits such as parental leave, family services, and day care. For the most part these policies address the lifestyle needs of mothers in the neotraditional and modern categories—those trying to balance work and family obligations. The costs of publicly subsidized day care are borne by all taxpayers, but the programs offer no benefits to childless women who prefer the postmodern lifestyle and are of little use to mothers outside the labor force who stay at home to care for their children. Indeed, childless women in full-time careers are rarely the subjects of family-related policy deliberations. One exception, noted earlier, is the case of childless workers in Germany who are being required to make higher contributions to the country's compulsory nursing-home insurance program than workers with children.

Compared to the industrial democracies of Europe, the United States is considered a laggard in dispensing parental leave, day care, and other publicly subsidized emollients to diminish the friction between raising a family and holding a job. The right to take twelve weeks of job-protected family leave was initiated in 1993, with coverage limited to companies with fifty employees or more—and the leave is unpaid. Although unpaid leave places no strain on the public coffer, there was a substantial rise in government spending on child care during the 1990s, which benefited mainly low-income families. Testifying before Congress in 2002, Douglas Besharov estimated that between 1994 and 1999 federal and state expenditures on child-care programs climbed by almost 60 percent, from $8.9 to $14.1 billion, most of which served low-income families.[1] About $2 billion of additional support was delivered to middle- and upper-income families through the child-care tax credit, for a total of $16 billion in publicly subsidized care.[2] While $16 billion is no trivial sum, it is still well below European expenditures on a per capita basis.

Spending on conventional family-friendly arrangements in the United States is relatively low, in part because of the ideological ambivalence in this realm of policy. Public sympathy for welfare programs that pay unmarried women to stay home and care for their children evaporated as the labor-force participation of married women with children under six years old multiplied threefold, from less than 20 percent in 1960 to more than 60 percent in 2000. Public spending on day care in the United States is largely related to making it possible for welfare mothers to enter the labor force. And conservatives have long argued for strengthening work requirements in welfare programs. At the same time, many conservatives also support the idea of "putting less emphasis on policies that free up parents to be better workers, and more emphasis on policies that free up workers to be better parents," as expressed in the Report to the Nation from the Commission on Children at Risk.[3] Liberals have traditionally resisted demands that welfare recipients should work for their benefits. But this position softens when gender feminists on the left advocate for universal child care and other policies that encourage all mothers to enter the paid workplace. Publicly subsidized child care is the most central and in many ways the most controversial provision in the standard package of benefits designed to harmonize work and family life.

Day Care: Substitute Mothering or Enhanced Development?

Most young children, even those with stay-at-home mothers, experience some nonmaternal care throughout the preschool years, ranging from an afternoon with grandparents to a few hours with a babysitter at home or at a play group in a local center. But these limited episodes are not sufficient to facilitate full-time participation in the labor force. Extended child care is the cornerstone of family-friendly policy. Without alternate care for thirty hours or more a week during the preschool years, two parents employed in regular full-time jobs would be unable to raise two children unless one of the working parents withdrew from the labor force for eight years.[4] Even then, a few hours of before- and after-school care would be necessary if both parents worked a regular nine-to-five shift or the longer hours of some high-powered professional firms.[5]

After-school programs that serve older children have excited less passion and received less attention in family-policy deliberations than programs that deliver extended, nonmaternal day care to preschoolers. Because the provision of extended preschool care diminishes the traditional role of motherhood during the early and critical childrearing years, it is hard to make a substantive assessment—positive or negative—of this service without hitting a sensitive nerve somewhere. Working mothers are distraught by studies that suggest they might be shortchanging their children by placing them in day care for long periods of time during the preschool years. And stay-at-home mothers are equally pained by studies suggesting that children in out-of-home care thrive more intellectually and socially than their own children, in whom they invest so much personal time and energy each day.

Research on the touchy subject of nonmaternal care and its interpretation in public discourse are further complicated by the blurring of two agendas, each with its own idea of what day care should achieve. One agenda is to furnish day care that serves as an equivalent substitute for the nurturing and socialization provided by an average mother. Following this course, day care serves mainly as a public provision to harmonize work and family life by permitting mothers to shift their labor to the market while ensuring that their children receive decent care that resembles acceptable standards of mothering. These programs are structured to accommodate the schedule of working parents, with early drop-offs, long hours, and late pick-ups.

The other agenda goes beyond supplying the care of an average substitute mother. It involves the provision of an enriching day-care experience that promises to improve on the socialization and academic skills that preschool children would otherwise acquire through maternal care. Here nonmaternal care aims not so much to help women balance motherhood and work as to help young children develop more fully than they might under the daily supervision of their mothers.

The agenda of developmental enhancement is usually associated with nonmaternal care directed toward children from disadvantaged families. These services are structured more to meet the social and educational needs of children than the work schedules of their parents. The largest and best known preschool program is Head Start, which usually runs for part of the day during nine months of the year.[6] One of Head Start's predecessors, the legendary Perry Preschool, was a model early-intervention program that ran thirty weeks of the year, with two-and-a-half-hour classes on weekday mornings and weekly one-and-a-half-hour home visits with mothers and children in the afternoon—a schedule hardly intended to facilitate the mothers' full-time employment.[7] One of the reasons sometimes given for the success of this program is that part of the intervention was aimed at parents.[8]

The two agendas of child care—enhanced development and substitute mothering—blur because they represent a continuum rather than two mutually exclusive alternatives. Substitute mothering seeks to provide an experience beyond mass-produced custodial care by offering the kind of intellectual stimulation and emotionally supportive interaction that children are expected to receive under healthy maternal care. On this side of the continuum, however, there are no doubt some services that approach custodial care, offering little more than warmth and safety. But child-care providers and parents rarely admit to it, claiming instead that these services fully meet the nurturing standards of substitute mothering. Developmental enhancement moves beyond substitute mothering. These services aim to deliver a more structured and advanced level of socialization and academic preparation than children would otherwise receive at home—giving them a "head start." All sorts of day-care arrangements along this continuum lay some claim to developmental benefits and insist that children thrive under their daily supervision. To do otherwise would put them out of business. Thus, the research and public discourse on these arrangements tend to concentrate on issues of developmental enhancement. Once the central question about the impact of nonmaternal care on child development is posed, there is always the incendiary possibility of uncovering detrimental effects.

Given the explosive potential of the subject, it is perhaps fortunate that much of the day-care research has been plagued by methodological flaws, resulting in a corpus of findings muffled by a host of qualifications that acknowledge selection bias, inconsistency of findings, lack of data on long-term effects, inability to measure subtle characteristics, and difficulty in establishing causality. In addition, there have been problems disentangling the complex interactions of numerous mediating variables—quality of care, number of hours in day care each day, maternal sensitivity, home environment, child's temperament, child's age, social class, father's involvement, mother's work schedule, child's sex, and number of children in the family, to mention the most obvious. A careful review of forty studies in the late 1970s concluded that knowledge about the effects of day care was exceedingly limited and that what was known could not be generalized to the kind and quality of care available throughout the country.[9]

Buffered by methodological qualifications, the first wave of child-care research in the 1970s and early 1980s avoided rattling the cage by making vague summary statements about the consequences of nonmaternal care and maternal home care, such as day care "typically does no harm," "children of working mothers do as well as those of mothers who stay at home," and "children of employed and non-employed mothers do not differ on various child adjustment measures."[10] Years later, in

1999, this theme was echoed in an American Psychological Association press release, which reported a study's conclusion that "having a working mother does no significant harm to children."[11] The findings attracted considerable media attention and were covered by the *CBS Evening News*, the *Washington Post*, and the *Atlanta Journal-Constitution*, among others. The media paid little attention to the fact that the findings were based on a sample of disproportionately low-income, single, young, minority mothers; it also ignored other details, including that the definition of "working" mothers lumped together those who worked a few hours a week with others who worked up to forty hours, and that the emotional assessments of the children were based primarily on what the mothers told government interviewers.[12]

The "does no harm" refrain was occasionally reinforced by child development experts, who asserted, for example, that "children are usually better off with a satisfied substitute care-giver and a happy part-time mother than with an angry frustrated full-time mother."[13] Statements along these lines conveyed the sense that nonmaternal care was an equivalent substitute provision for traditional mothering—while implicitly encouraging bored, frustrated mothers suffering from Friedan's problem with no name to join the female exodus into the labor market, which was in high gear at the time.

These quantitative studies in the 1970s and 1980s were usually bland and reassuring; however, qualitative assessments of nonmaternal care, which looked at how children experience life in these settings on a daily basis, offered a more discomforting view. Deborah Fallows's appraisal of the day-care experience found a cheerless, desultory milieu in most of the facilities she observed around the country. Fallows described the quality of a child's daily existence in a typical day-care center, where the main activity was filling time: "He didn't do badly—he roamed independently, joining in when he felt like it, taking off when he didn't. He got no individual attention, because he didn't demand any. He got no special instruction, because none was offered. No one talked to him or hugged him, because there weren't enough adults to go around."[14] There were exceptions, of course, the best of which were very pricey.

Seeking to address some of the weaknesses in earlier studies, a new wave of rigorous empirical research was launched in the early 1990s, starting with the National Institute of Child Health and Human Development's (NICHD) Study of Early Child Care. This large-scale longitudinal investigation followed an initial sample of 1,364 children from birth through age seven in ten vicinities across the United States. The study was conducted by the NICHD Early Child Care Research Network—a team of twenty-five researchers from ten universities. Members of the research network and other scholars given access to the NICHD data generated a voluminous body of empirical work analyzing connections among developmental outcomes and a wide range of variables such as the quality of the child-care environment, the quality of the school environment (as the children entered kindergarten and the primary grades), and the quality of home and family life.[15]

The NICHD study is one of the most exacting and comprehensive of its kind to date, described by child development experts as the gold standard in this area of research.[16] Despite such praise, however, the survey methods used to produce the findings discussed below are subject to the type of criticism often brought to bear on nonexperimental studies (that is, studies that do not employ a rigorous experimental design, which involves random assignment of subjects to experimental and control groups).[17] The NICHD researchers studied child care from an instrumental perspective, focusing on the results of nonmaternal care. The outcomes most frequently brought to the public's attention analyzed the effects of quality care on attachment relationships with mothers, behavioral problems, and cognitive development. Although the numbers were clear and the statistics conveyed a voice of scientific authority, their meaning was open to interpretation.

Regarding the emotional bond between mothers and children, psychologists believe that the security of the mother-child attachment in the early years exerts a measurable influence on the child's feelings about self and others, and on the child's future capacity to form relationships and regulate aggression. Prior to the NICHD research there was heated discussion about child care's potentially negative impact on the mother-child attachment. In the late 1970s, for example, Selma Fraiberg expressed concern that this bond would be seriously impaired by placing youngsters in extended child care. She worried that children in day care would be subjected to the rough justice of the preschool playground, while learning "that all adults are interchangeable, that love is capricious, that human attachment is a perilous investment, and that love should be hoarded for the self in the service of survival."[18] But in an initial systematic review of the empirical research literature, Jay Belsky, a highly respected psychology professor, and his colleagues found little evidence that day care for infants had detrimental effects on the mother-child bond.[19] Later, however, Belsky reexamined the evidence and found it more troubling. He concluded, with painstaking caution, "that if one does not feel compelled to draw only irrefutable conclusions, a relatively persuasive *circumstantial* case can be made that early infant care *may* be associated with the increased avoidance of mother, *possibly* to the point of greater insecurity in the attachment relationship, and that such care *may* also be associated with diminished compliance and cooperation with adults, increased aggressiveness, and possibly even greater social maladjustment in the preschool and early school-age years" (emphasis in original).[20] This statement was made in the mid-1980s, when the research evidence rarely controlled for child-care quality and family differences.

By the mid-1990s, the NICHD study was able to conduct more sophisticated analyses using information on the quality of care and family differences. Revisiting the issue of mother-child attachment, the NICHD found that extended nonmaternal child care was not linked to increased insecurity, except in those instances where maternal sensitivity and quality of child care were judged to be low. Maternal sensitivity was measured in terms of the mothers' expressions of supportiveness, intrusiveness, positive regard, and hostility observed in videotaped interactions with their children. Quality of child care was assessed according to structural characteristics, such as the caregiver-child ratio and the number of children under supervision, as well as the caregivers' training, education, and behavior, such as language stimulation and emotionally supportive interactions. The NICHD research showed that the likelihood of insecure mother-child attachment at fifteen months increased when children were in nonmaternal care more than ten hours per week *only* for those children whose mothers were judged as highly insensitive and who received a low quality of care.[21] A similar finding was observed at thirty-six months.[22]

The good news is that when the data are controlled for quality and maternal sensitivity, extended child care does not appear to diminish the security of attachment. But this assessment starts to waver a bit in light of further analyses. First, when evaluating the quality of nonmaternal child care in centers against the guidelines of the American Public Health Association and the American Academy of Pediatrics, the NICHD research team found that "the results were not encouraging."[23] Other studies of 628 centers gave an overall average quality rating of a little less than halfway between minimal and good.[24] Not only is most child care of mediocre quality, but it was also found that mothers who were judged as less sensitive were more likely to have children in centers where the quality of care was not highly rated.[25] Finally, mothers who were judged low on the measures of maternal sensitivity tended to have children who spent more hours in nonmaternal care.[26]

The web of cause-and-effect relationships among mother-child attachment, family characteristics such as maternal sensitivity, and quantity and quality of nonmaternal care is difficult to untangle. The issue depends in part on whether maternal insensitivity is seen as an inherent personal characteristic or as a reaction to broader circumstances. Women employed full-time necessarily have children who spend extended periods in nonmaternal care. Under the stress of trying to balance full-time employment and motherhood, it is possible that these mothers will be less relaxed, patient, tolerant, and responsive in interactions with their children—thus scoring lower in maternal sensitivity—than mothers who are not as pressed in their daily lives. In these circumstances the association between maternal insensitivity and extended time in child care might well stem from the antecedent condition of full-time employment. Since the quality of most day-care services tends to be no more than mediocre, even those who want and can afford high-quality care have a hard time finding it. Thus, although child care per se poses little threat to mother-child attachment, given the current attributes of child-care offerings in the United States, children under three years of age in extended nonmaternal care on average probably have a somewhat higher risk of developing insecure attachments than those cared for by mothers at home.

In contrast to the weak link between the amount of time spent in nonmaternal care during the preschool years and the security of the mother-child attachment, the NICHD study revealed a comparatively robust relationship between the amount of time spent in nonmaternal care during the preschool years and the likelihood of behavioral problems, particularly aggressive behavior toward other children, showing up in kindergarten.[27] Specifically, the research found that children in regularly scheduled nonmaternal care more than thirty hours per week during the first four and a half years of life were almost three times more likely to behave aggressively toward other children than children who had been in nonmaternal care less than ten hours per week. Although the difference sounds quite large, in absolute terms it represents a gap of 11 percentage points—between problematic behavior expressed by 17 percent of children who were in extended nonmaternal care and by 6 percent of children who were in nonmaternal care for shorter periods of time. Another way of interpreting the results is to highlight the good news that behavioral problems were not evident in 83 percent of children in extended care.[28]

The apparent impact of extended care was moderate, but not trivial. Further analyses lend increasing credibility to these findings. The data showed not merely a simple correlation between quantity of care and behavioral problems but a more compelling "dose-response" relationship. That is, the average scores on problem behavior rose consistently with the amount of time children spent in nonmaternal care.[29] Moreover, the relationship between quantity of care and problem behavior remained significant even after controlling for the quality and type of care, and for family background.[30] It is possible, however, that selection bias might have accounted for the higher levels of aggressive behavior among those in extended care, if rambunctious and difficult-to-manage children were more likely to be placed in care centers for longer hours than placid and easy-to-manage kids.

Does it really make much difference if the behavior of children who spend an extended period in day care is more problematic than that of other children when they enter kindergarten? The answer depends, in part, upon whether this result is judged from an existential or instrumental perspective. From an existential perspective, how children experience life on a daily basis is as important as future outcomes. In this view, the understanding of a good life is based on what takes place during the journey as much as the eventual destination. Thus, the existentialists' answer is yes, the higher level of aggressive behavior matters, since it would make kindergarten a less pleasant experience in the voyage of life for both the kids who act out and their classmates. From an instrumental perspective, concerns are more sharply focused on the long-term impact of extended day care on cognitive and behavioral outcomes. Instrumentalists want to know what the aggressive behavior in kindergarten will lead to—will the aggressive kids grow up to be thugs or captains of industry? Or will they simply mellow out over time?

In fact, the children did eventually mellow out. The data show that when the children were evaluated after kindergarten, the earlier relationship between the quantity of early child care and levels of problem behavior began to dissipate, and by the third grade it was no longer statistically significant. These findings at the third-grade level do not close the book, since effects associated with early child care that seemed to disappear have been found to reemerge later, particularly during periods of developmental transitions. As the study's authors caution, "It remains to be determined if these relations with early child care remain, dissipate or grow in early adolescence, a critical transition period for many children."[31]

While behavioral problems associated with extended child care regardless of quality were no longer evident by the third grade, findings from the NICHD study showed that academic gains were linked to high-quality care and were sustained through the third grade.[32] These findings are supported by other large-sample studies.[33] In most cases, however, the gains were modest in size and had the largest impact on vulnerable children from disadvantaged families.[34] And there is also some evidence that academic gains associated with preschool attendance fade over the early years of elementary school.[35] Still, several of the model early-intervention programs, such as Perry Preschool and the Carolina Abecedarian program, showed promising long-term results. Coming from very deprived backgrounds, the Perry Preschool participants were more likely to have graduated from high school and to be employed by age nineteen, and to earn more, have fewer criminal arrests, and receive less welfare by age twenty-eight, than the control group.[36]

No doubt, there is a good case to be made for providing extended nonmaternal care to seriously disadvantaged children from homes that fail to offer sufficient cognitive stimulation and emotional support or that present high risks of abuse and neglect. Yet, for a variety of reasons, such as limited education, social problems, and psychological deficiencies, mothers from these homes are least likely to find employment that would pay for the costs of such care. (Ironically, some of these women could conceivably become child-care workers, earning a median hourly wage of $8.06.)[37]

But the vast majority of young children in the United States are not from disadvantaged families. Their life experiences are shaped by competent mothers (over 80 percent of whom have at least completed high school) whose nurturing and personal interactions are vested with more devotion than money can buy. These children are least likely to gain substantial or persistent social and cognitive benefits from high-quality nonmaternal care. Indeed, cut through the professional jargon of "structure" (small groups with a high ratio of caretakers to children) and "processes" (language stimulation and positive reinforcement), and you find that the essential definition of high-quality day care approximates the warm, personal, and supportive interactions associated with average maternal care. There is much evidence that family characteristics, particularly mother's education, have considerably more effect than day-care experiences on cognitive development and other outcomes.[38] And there are some indications that children from well-functioning, middle-class families, particularly males, may be disadvantaged by nonmaternal care.[39]

What does all this tell us about the consequences of extended day care as a family-friendly policy? In trying to understand the impact of day care it is helpful to distinguish between programs that offer substitute mothering designed to mind preschool children during their parents' working hours and those that offer special services designed to enhance children's cognitive and emotional development beyond what they would normally receive at home. Overall, the research suggests that the emotional, behavioral, and cognitive effects of nonmaternal day care are mixed and vary depending on the intensity and quality of the service as well as the characteristics of the children and their families. Neither the advantages nor the detrimental effects appear to be large, and both fade over time to some extent. A few of the most costly and well-executed programs intended to enhance development have shown promising long-term results, predominantly for children from socially and economically disadvantaged families. It is important to recognize, however, that while these programs offer potential benefits for children in vulnerable circumstances, for the most part they do not provide the extended hours of care that are necessary to facilitate the parents' full-time employment.

In sum, after more than thirty years of research we have gained a deeper appreciation of the complexities of gauging how extended child care affects children, but our conclusions remain in limbo. There is little evidence that these programs benefit the daily experiences or enhance the developmental capacities of most children who are not highly disadvantaged. At the same time there is no convincing evidence that these programs have long-lasting detrimental effects. Given the uncertain impact on children, all that can be said for extended day care as a family friendly policy is that it is most friendly to mothers who want or are required by dire necessity to work long hours outside the home.

Family Policy: Promoting Mothers or Markets?

What about the benefits of the broader package of conventional family-friendly policies generally available in the major industrialized democracies? To whom or what are they friendly? Western European countries are well known for having a more powerful arsenal of day care and other family-friendly benefits than the United States. For example, more than 70 percent of the children from age three to school age in Belgium, Denmark, France, Germany, Italy, the Netherlands, and the United Kingdom are in publicly financed child care.[40] Paid maternity leave, long periods of vacation, and government allowances for children and families are also common.

But the high levels of public care and other benefits have not been matched by the private production of children. Indeed, in a number of European nations, the birthrate is perched on the brink of demographic suicide. At the current level of decline, Belgium's native-born population is poised to fall by 12.5 percent between 2001 and 2020. Spain's population is expected to plunge by almost 25 percent over the next forty-five years, and during that time Germany is also expected to suffer a huge population loss, comparable to the size of the population of the former East Germany.[41] No member nation of the European Union currently has a fertility rate high enough to replace their existing population (replacement level is 2.1). And United Nations projections show the fertility rate remaining well below the replacement level through 2050.

The shrinking of native-born populations between 2005 and 2050 could be offset somewhat by the movement of an estimated 98 million international migrants from underdeveloped regions of the world.[42] However, absorption of that many outsiders could result in the transformation, if not the collapse, of established cultures. Beyond jeopardizing the cultural heritage of nations, declining birthrates have a ripple effect on family life. Fewer people experience being fathers and mothers, having brothers and sisters, being grandparents or aunts and uncles. As the web of intergenerational family relationships withers, generating less social, emotional, and fiscal support, the state comes under greater pressure to provide public services for what was previously handled in private life.

It is possible that low fertility rates will start to climb without any outside intervention, particularly under conditions in which immigration is tightly controlled. The well-known Easterlin hypothesis suggests that as fertility declines, individual opportunities increase, along with personal welfare. Compared to the previous cohort, those born into a low-fertility society encounter, for example, fewer people competing for jobs in the labor market, more houses for sale to fewer available buyers, and a relatively higher number of slots in the educational system. The increasing level of opportunity and personal welfare presumably lowers the costs of having children.[43] However, Easterlin's economic perspective on fertility has been challenged on various fronts. Opposing arguments suggest that social attitudes may influence childbearing behavior more than economic costs and benefits, and that societal conditions have changed in recent decades, which may have diminished the self-correcting effect of cohort size on fertility.[44]

At the same time that fertility rates have declined, female labor-force participation and divorce rates have increased throughout the European Union. The temporal connection between women entering the labor force and having fewer children is open to various interpretations based on the time frames selected, the countries included in the analysis, the statistical manipulations applied to the data, and what one is looking to prove. The exactitude of measurement is also worth bearing in mind—the European Union labor-force survey defines as "employed" all respondents who report at least *one hour* of gainful employment in the previous week.

Contrary to what one might expect, sociologist Gosta Esping-Andersen found that in 1992 European countries with high levels of female employment tended to have higher fertility rates than those with low levels of female employment. This was a reversal of the negative relationship between fertility and employment found among those countries in earlier years. Based on a positive correlation from a cross-sectional analysis of nineteen countries, he concluded that in some contexts women's careers and children can become fairly compatible.[45] Similar moderately positive results emerged from a cross-sectional analysis of fertility rates and female employment in twelve European countries in 1997.[46] In both instances, it is worth noting that the countries that registered the highest fertility rates were still well below the replacement level.

In reality, these positive findings say more about the perspective afforded by cross-sectional analysis than about the overall long-term trend in the relationship between fertility and female labor-force participation rates. Repeated cross-sectional analyses comparing different countries at various points in time over several decades show that the negative correlation between fertility rates and female employment was reversed by the 1990s. From a longitudinal perspective, however, fertility rates declined as female employment increased in each country—but the magnitude of this negative association became weaker over time.[47]

Among the forces that might affect the relationship between changes in fertility and female employment, Esping-Andersen suggests that we would be likely to find a positive influence in countries where day care and family services are offered to everyone. Sweden, Finland, and Denmark are among the countries where these services are most widely available. They also have among the highest fertility rates in the European Union. Yet, in each of these countries, female labor-force participation rates were higher in 2004 than in 1994 while fertility rates were lower in 2004 than in 1994 (see Appendix, Table 1). This inverse relationship presents a completely different picture than the positive one that emerges from a cross-sectional perspective. Indeed, taking a larger group of countries (seventeen) over a longer period of time (1980 to 2002), we find a substantial inverse relationship between the average fertility and female employment rates. But there are several ways to look at these data, and different results appear depending on how the analysis is framed (see Appendix, Figures 1, 2, and 3).

Following the downward trend in fertility, a corresponding decline in marriage rates between 1980 and 2001 shows a strong inverse correlation with female labor-force participation (see Appendix, Figure 4). Much of the decline in marriage has been made up for by the historic increase in cohabitation across northern Europe. From Scandinavia to France the formality of marriage has fallen out of favor with a huge proportion of the current generation. By 2005 more than half of all first-born French children had unwed parents, most of whom were in an ongoing relationship. The normative acceptance of this shift away from the traditional commitment of marriage is reflected by the long-term cohabitations of such popular political figures as Segolene Royal, the French Socialist Party's 2007 presidential candidate, and François Hollande, the party's leader, who lived together for twenty-five years; and Defense Minister Michèle Alliot-Marie, who is in a long-term relationship with a member of the National Assembly.[48]

As female labor-force participation rates climbed, public efforts were made to reduce the friction between work and family life in many of the advanced industrialized countries of the OECD. One way to estimate the effects of these efforts is to look at how patterns of public spending on family-friendly benefits such as day care, household services, maternity and parental leave, children's allowances, and other social provisions vary with marriage and fertility rates. Although the pattern of spending on family-friendly benefits rises and falls, overall the average rates of public expenditure on these benefits as a percentage of GDP increased slightly between 1980 and 2001 (see Appendix, Figure 5). This spending had an inverse correlation with fertility rates and showed a similar relationship to marriage rates.

Findings based on aggregate data may, of course, mask large variations between individual countries and among groups of countries. Analysis conducted on countries grouped according to the widely cited classification of social-democratic, conservative, liberal, and southern European regimes showed some variance from the pattern that emerged when the results for all countries were averaged.[49] Specifically, a positive correlation appeared between fertility rates and spending on family benefits in the social-democratic Scandinavian countries. The social-democratic countries also had a higher level of public expenditure on family-friendly benefits than other groups. After 1990, however, social-democratic expenditures began to decline while the levels of spending in other regimes increased or remained constant, causing the average spending on family-friendly benefits to converge.[50] A case might be made that too much attention to levels of spending on family-friendly measures ignores important differences in the substantive configuration of these policies, which influence work and family relations.[51] Indeed, even among the social-democratic Scandinavian countries, sharp differences emerge in the extent to which family policies promote gender equality and afford mothers the right to choose among alternative child-care arrangements.[52]

Family-friendly policies, of course, involve more than the OECD categories of expenditure represented by family benefits. For example, more than 70 percent of the employed women in the Netherlands work in part-time jobs that have benefits similar to those of full-time employment, and Dutch children spend more days per year in school than most elementary school students in the European Union. A thorough assessment of the measures that affect efforts to balance work and family life would include flexible work schedules, number and length of school days, paid vacation time, and other benefits, some of which are reflected in the larger scheme of total public social expenditures.[53] Analyses of overall social-expenditure data reveal patterns that parallel the findings noted above—that is, rates of total public social expenditure between 1980 and 2001 are inversely related to both fertility and marriage rates (see Appendix, Figure 6).

Still, even when total public social expenditures are considered the picture is not complete, since there are different ways to count public spending. A caveat on comparative data is in order. It has long been recognized that, in addition to the checks written directly by government, comprehensive measures of social-welfare efforts should include other sources of social expenditure that promote individual well-being. In the 1930s, special tax deductions and exemptions were identified as a form of government aid in Arthur Pigou's classic text *Economics of Welfare*. It was not until the mid-1970s, however, that data on tax expenditures became available and were introduced as a regular component of the president's budget in the United States.[54] In the 1980s it became increasingly clear that the conventional categories of social expenditure were at best a crude metric for comparisons among different countries.[55] In the mid-1990s, as additional data came available, researchers at the OECD developed a new ledger for social accounting, which controls for the effects of costs and benefits from various sources.[56] Yet even this highly sophisticated measure does not take into account the effects of government deficit spending, which can finance current benefits through the creation of debt that must be discharged sometime in the future.

Moreover, the most sophisticated measure of net social expenditure, which compares spending among countries as a percentage of their GDP, yields a different set of results than when assessments are based on spending per capita. An analysis of social-welfare spending among ten OECD countries reveals that when the measurement shifts from the size of expenditure as a percentage of GDP to the size of per capita expenditure, the United States' rank jumps from near the bottom (just above Canada and Australia) to second from the top (just below Sweden).[57] All of these cautions about comparative measurements are to say that the findings that fertility and marriage rates have often declined as spending on family benefits and total social expenditure have increased can only be taken as suggestive. But what do they suggest?

Believers, Skeptics, and Disbelievers

These findings lend themselves to at least three broad interpretations, representing those who believe in the salutary effects of family-friendly policies, those who are skeptical, and those who disbelieve. It is clear that increased family-friendly provisions have not reversed whatever forces—economic, normative, social/psychological—are driving fertility rates down to below replacement levels. Believers would argue, however, that although such policies do not appear to strengthen the formation of family life (by increasing the presence of children and marriage), without these benefits the declines would have been even sharper—that is, they believe these benefits acted as a brake to slow things down. As evidence, they might point to the positive correlations between fertility rates and public expenditure on family benefits that were found in Scandinavian countries where levels of expenditure were proportionately more than twice as high as in most other OECD countries.

Although fertility rates remain below the replacement level, the Scandinavian experience suggests that the decline can be diminished if significant resources are invested in family services. On the issue of whether family policies are a remedy to low fertility rates in European countries, Gerda Neyer concludes, "Countries which regard their family policies as part of labor-market policies, of care policies, and of gender policies, seem to have retained fertility above the lowest-low levels. They use strategies directed at changing the labor market so that both men and women are able to maintain employment and income, even if they have (small) children to care for."[58]

But if these policies serve as a brake on declining rates of fertility, one would expect to find the lowest fertility rates in countries that lag behind in the provision of family-friendly benefits—the United States being a prime example. In comparison to the comprehensive package of public supports to reconcile work and family responsibilities in European countries, the pervasive view is that "American public policy leaves the vast majority of working parents high and dry."[59] So what accounts for the curiously high fertility rate in the United States? It is not the result of elevated birthrates among immigrants and minorities. Although higher birthrates in these groups account for part of the fertility gap between the United States and Europe, in 2004 the total fertility rate of the non-Hispanic white majority in the United States was 1.85—well above the rate of all the European Union countries, except Ireland and France (and part of the high rate in France is attributed to their large Muslim population).

Instead, some believers have claimed that as in Scandinavian countries, conditions in the United States (such as a flexible job market and the availability of child care) actually minimize the incompatibility between the childrearing demands of motherhood and paid employment for women—appearances notwithstanding. The flexible nature of the U.S. job market is seen as highly conducive to combining work and family life by affording schedules that permit dual-earner couples to stagger their working hours so that at least one of them can be at home at any given time.[60] This explanation of the U.S. experience would strike many family-policy researchers as a bit of a stretch, since they rarely find the American business community all that responsive to the needs of working mothers. Janet Gornick and Marcia Meyers claim, for example, that working conditions in the United States are less family friendly than in Europe because U.S. workers are more likely to encounter choices "between forty-hour-a-week employment and no employment or between mandatory overtime and losing their jobs."[61] Joan Williams argues persuasively that women are held to the male model of the "ideal worker," whose schedule sanctions no compromise with family demands.[62] Still, there are indications of a market response to the increased proportion of employed mothers as some workplaces institute more flexible work hours and expand the scope of paid sick leave to include children's illnesses.[63]

In terms of nonmaternal day care, believers contend that while public provision is relatively limited, "the United States provides an example of business and voluntary organizations increasing the availability of child care."[64] Day care is seen as more acceptable in the United States than in countries with lower fertility rates; for example, according to surveys, Germans agreed more frequently than Americans with the idea that children suffer if their mothers go to work. The believer reasons that the relatively high U.S. fertility rates "must lie in the responsiveness of nongovernmental institutions," which reinforces the idea that, whether public or private, day care and other family-friendly arrangements significantly influence childbearing decisions.[65]

Invoking the mantra "Correlation is not causality," skeptics find little reason to assume that these policies are either friendly or unfriendly to families and read the results as confirming that family-friendly policies make no palpable difference. The two-variable equation of family policy and fertility excludes many relevant factors, such as employment rates, cultural traditions, and cohabitation. Scandinavian countries with comparatively high fertility rates also have the highest level cohabitation in the European Union—some researchers have found a relationship between cohabitation and fertility rates.[66] In addition, the resources of the extended family do not enter the formal accounting of family-policy expenditures. In Italy and Greece, more than 25 percent of grandparents age fifty and over are engaged in providing free child care for four hours or more a day.[67]

Skeptics would no doubt recall the history of children's allowances in France, which were initiated under the Family Code of 1939 with explicit pro-natalist objectives. Although the French birthrate increased considerably in the decades after World War II, the birthrate in the United States—which had no children's allowance—also rose dramatically during the same period, while the birthrate in Sweden declined despite its allowance system.[68] As for more recent empirical evidence, skeptics would concur with Joelle Sleebos's assessment that the findings from forty-two multivariate studies on family-friendly policies are often inconclusive and contradictory. The current state of knowledge about the impact of these policies is too limited to guide effective public intervention.[69]

Skeptics reason that decisions concerning marriage and family size address fundamental values of human existence, which do not yield readily to social policy. Thus, they would argue that while no single factor is definitive, the differences in support for traditional values and beliefs has a significant bearing on the gap in fertility rates between the United States and Europe. Data comparing religious values in Europe and the United States showed that Americans were almost three times as likely to say that God was very important in their lives and twice as likely to participate in religious activity as the average person in the fourteen European countries surveyed. In addition, 59 percent of U.S. respondents attended religious service at least once a month in contrast to 10 percent in Sweden, 13 percent in Norway, and 17 percent in France. These striking differences convey a palpable sense of the extent to which people in the United States hold more traditional values and beliefs than typical Europeans (see Appendix, Table 2).[70]

A one-variable explanation, however, rarely captures the full range of complex interactions that account for people's decisions to bring children into the world—even when the variable is as powerful as the influence of religious belief. Although Ireland and the United States registered the highest support for religious values and had among the highest fertility rates, Italy came in third just behind them on support for religious values yet had one of the lowest fertility rates in Europe.[71]

Finally, in contrast to both believers and skeptics, disbelievers conclude that so-called family-friendly policies are not really family friendly at all. Rather, they argue that although the historical patterns that show female labor-force participation and expenditures on family benefits rising as fertility and marriage rates decline do not represent definitive explanations, they are indicative of two firm underlying realities.

First, for the vast majority of people there is no way to "harmonize" the demands of working at a full-time job, raising children, and managing a household. "Harmony" is a euphemism for surviving the pandemonium of daily life under those circumstances. As any woman who has tried it can testify, efforts to balance paid work and family life demand extraordinary physical exertion and personal sacrifice during the early childhood years. Caring for young children is immensely labor intensive and relentless. Most who do it survive, but under the best of circumstances—high-quality day care, low-keyed children, and a helpful partner—few engaged in the struggle would characterize the life of a working mother with young children as harmonious.

A two-earner family with two children under five years of age hits the ground running just before sunrise. The kids have to be washed, fed, dressed, and herded out the door in time to get to the day-care center well before the parents are due at their jobs. At 5:00 p.m., the parents leave work, rush to pick up the kids, and take them home to be fed, undressed, bathed, and put to bed. This tight daily routine can be further squeezed by jobs that require evening meetings, out-of-town travel, overtime, and take-home work. On top of that, parents must find time for grocery shopping, buying children's clothes, housecleaning, doing laundry, going to doctor appointments, and getting haircuts—in addition to coping with pinkeye, strep throat, and ear infections that regularly strike without warning. It does not take much for things to spin out of control: a dead car battery, a broken washing machine, or a leaky roof will do it.

Although many men have increased their involvement in domestic life, whether due to nature or nurture they still do far less than their fair share of traditional female duties. The hard reality is that most working mothers continue to assume the brunt of household and child-care responsibilities. Even if, as some feminists wish, this were to change drastically so that fathers shouldered a full 50 percent of the domestic chores and childrearing duties, family life would still be no picnic. Some people manage it better than others. Those who do it best usually have high energy, a lot of money, and some spry grandparents nearby to lend a hand. For everyone else, no matter how fairly the work is divided, the normal obligations of two full-time work careers and two children under five years old leave little time or space in which to harmonize the daily rhythms of life. And despite all the working mother's efforts, at the end of each week her young children will have spent the majority of their waking hours having their physical needs met and their personalities shaped by strangers.

The second reality is that the main threads of family-friendly policies are tied to and reinforce female labor-force participation—a more apt label would be "market friendly." Since the late 1990s, as Jane Lewis explains, family policy in the European Union "has been explicitly linked to the promotion of women's employment in order to further the economic growth and competition agenda."[72] These work-oriented policies are largely, though not entirely, associated with publicly provided care for children and supports for periods of parental leave. To qualify for parental-leave benefits it is necessary to have a job before having children. The incentive for early attachment to the labor force is bolstered by publicly subsidized day care. Child-care services both compensate for the absence of parental child care in families with working mothers and generate an economic spur for mothers to shift their labor from the home to the market. In Sweden, for example, free day-care services are state-subsidized by as much as $11,900 per child.[73] They are free at the point of consumption but paid for dearly by direct and indirect taxes. In 1990, Swedish taxes absorbed the highest proportion of the gross domestic product of any OECD country. Paying in advance for the "free" day-care service tends to squeeze mothers into the labor force, since the crushing tax rates make it difficult for an average family to get by on a single salary.

As noted earlier, most of the employed Swedish women end up working in the public sector. By Patricia Morgan's reckoning, not only are women's employment opportunities in Sweden less equal than those of women in the United States, the United Kingdom, and Germany, but Sweden "is more gender-segregated than Asian countries like China, Hong Kong and India."[74] In Scandinavia the traditional women's work of socializing children and caring for the sick is still done by women, but it is now performed for a government wage rather than for the intimate and sympathetic commitments of family life. Alan Wolfe discerns that "the Scandinavian welfare states which express so well a sense of obligation to distant strangers, are beginning to make it more difficult to express a sense of obligation to those with whom one shares family ties."[75] Still in all fairness, as David Popenoe argues, "in a strict comparison, Scandinavia is probably preferable to the United States today as a place to raise young children."[76] Not only is Sweden more culturally homogenous, it also is a less individualistic and consumer-oriented society than the United States. And almost all

Swedish mothers are subsidized to stay at home with their infants for the first year.

The disbeliever argues that for many people, if not most, the quality of family life suffers when mothers with young children go to work; hence, policies that create incentives to shift informal labor invested in child care and domestic production to the realm of paid employment are not "family friendly" in a universal sense. From this perspective, there is a meaningful connection between the decline in marriage and fertility and the increased investments in family benefits in recent decades.

Seen in the context of women's diverse interests in work and family life, each of the interpretations outlined above frames a slice of reality; that is, the consequences of family-friendly policies vary in strength and direction for women with different lifestyle preferences. The skeptic is correct in the sense that these policies probably have little effect on women at the two ends of the work-family continuum—those who prefer the traditional and postmodern lifestyles. Just as the availability of subsidized child-care services is unlikely to redirect those postmodern women who are firmly dedicated to a professional career and really not interested in having children, it is doubtful that most traditional women disposed toward rearing three or more children would be seriously influenced by the prospect of having their children cared for on a daily basis by other people.

Although there is some elasticity within each lifestyle category, the largest potential for movement is among the neo-traditional and modern lifestyles of those women somewhere in the middle of the continuum. On one hand, the believer probably has a point in that child care and other family benefits facilitate the lifestyle objectives of some women in the modern group—those who want a child but are work oriented and inclined to limit family size. In the absence of family benefits, the increased difficulty of rearing children while actively pursuing a career might have a dampening effect on fertility and marriage rates among these women—some of whom might move into the postmodern lifestyle. On the other hand, the disbeliever's view that most family-friendly policies undermine the institution they are purported to support probably resonates with some women in the neotraditional group for whom work is secondary to child care. In the absence of family benefits that create incentives to work and lend impetus to the normative devaluation of childrearing and the domestic arts, fertility rates might rise as some women disposed toward a neotraditional lifestyle gravitated into the traditional category.

It is fair to say that family policies can be friendlier to some lifestyles than to others—they support the personal interests and psychological ambitions of some, but not all, women. Recognition of this diversity underscores the social obligation of policy makers to explore alternatives to the conventional package of public benefits that are supposed to help women balance work and family life.

Conclusion: An Alternative to the Male Model

Chapter VI
Rethinking Family Policy

Among academics, journalists, politicians, feminist leaders, and almost everyone else whose opinions on the role of modern-day women are in print, there is widespread agreement that something must be done to harmonize work and family life. As to the best approach, the overwhelming majority back two courses of action—the adoption of so-called family-friendly policies and of gender-neutralizing policies.

The first and most popular approach encompasses a range of public and private measures, starting most notably with the provision of subsidized, high-quality nonmaternal child care, which allow mothers with young children to be able to work.[1] Regarding this course, the United States is often advised by family-policy analysts to follow Europe's lead and has indeed been moving in that direction.[2] Between 1994 and 1999, public spending on child care in the United States shot up by 60 percent, as previously noted. More recently, David Kirp detected a universal preschool movement taking off, with Oklahoma, of all the unlikely places, in the lead—63 percent of the state's four-year-olds were in public preschool programs in 2004. At the same time, 57 percent of Georgia's four-year-olds were in preschool programs, and a serious bid to introduce universal preschool was being entertained in Florida.[3] In 2006, however, a referendum to introduce universal preschool in California was roundly defeated. Currently, the stirrings of a universal preschool movement in the United States are faint but palpable.

After early child care, paid parental leave and part-time work schedules are most frequently endorsed as mechanisms needed to balance motherhood and active labor-force participation. The Netherlands, for example, has made considerable efforts to stimulate and regulate part-time employment. More than one-third of Dutch workers have a part-time job, giving the Netherlands the highest level of part-time employment in Europe. Women hold 67 percent of these jobs.[4]

Far-reaching statutory measures are complemented by more-circumscribed voluntary workplace policies such as flexible working hours, access to a telephone for family-related calls, and special family leave.[5] Specific policies are often tailored to assist women on the fast track to high-powered careers in law firms, universities, hospitals, and other professional sectors of the private market. For most women aiming high, the road to commanding positions in the administrative power structure of Fortune 500 companies, partnerships in elite law firms and medical practices, tenured faculty posts at research universities, and influential media posts begins in graduate school. At the University of California, for example, family-friendly initiatives for graduate students include providing day-care facilities for toddlers, extending the period of time for the completion of course work, and offering paid maternity leave for students who receive university support.

Faculty get a somewhat heftier package of benefits, such as excused leave from the tenure clock for up to two years, a part-time option, paid maternity leave, and modified work responsibilities that provide paid relief from all teaching duties for up to two semesters.[6] (However, university benefits such as the two-semester paid relief from work do not extend to secretaries, administrative assistants, janitorial staff, and others not on the tenure track.)

The second conventional approach involves policies aimed at reducing if not completely eliminating gender-role differentiation in family life and the labor market. Along with the drive for family-friendly policies, there is ubiquitous support for measures to advance gender equality as a means of reconciling motherhood and paid employment. Increasing gender equality in domestic tasks, and most importantly in childrearing, is seen as a way to relieve mothers of some of the burden of unpaid family labor so that they can devote more time and energy to their careers. It is widely accepted that in dual-earner families, the struggle to balance work and family life should be more equally distributed between parents. This approach is promoted by rules and incentives designed to modify traditional gender roles. Thus, the OECD counsels that social benefits should be structured to "carry the same incentives for both sexes with regard to the division of time between paid employment, domestic duties, and leisure."[7]

Efforts to balance policy-generated incentives for mothers and fathers are most evident in maternity-leave reform. Not only have many maternity-leave systems been transformed into parental leave, which can be taken by both fathers and mothers, but in recent years Denmark, Norway, and Italy have introduced reforms under which one month of parental leave is restricted to use only by fathers. Portugal's policy of parental leave has a "father quota" of fifteen days.[8] Iceland's policy of parental leave generates a forceful "use it or lose it" incentive, with three months of leave allocated strictly to fathers (in addition, three months are allocated to mothers, and another three months can be shared as the parents wish). In contrast to the "use it or lose it" policies, which significantly diminish the amount of parental leave for families if fathers do not participate, in Finland fathers who take the last twelve days of parental leave receive a bonus of twelve extra days of leave.[9]

To what extent have these various incentives induced men to assume a greater share of child-care responsibility? On this issue, the Swedish experience is informative. With one of the best known and most generous systems of parental leave, Sweden has been at the forefront of efforts to increase fathers' involvement in child care. After a 1995 reform, the Swedish system provided 360 days of parental leave at 80 percent of the parent's salary, plus another 90 days reimbursed at a flat rate of approximately eight dollars a day. The centerpiece of this reform required that at least one month of leave had to be taken by each of the parents. Since there was really no need to urge mothers to take advantage of this benefit, the obligatory leave became known as the "daddy month."

The Swedish government expected the daddy month to alter the division of child-care labor to create "a more even distribution of interruptions in work between men and women" (echoing the perception of childrearing as an "interruption" in employment, noted in Chapter 4).[10] An analysis comparing the use of parental leave immediately before and after the 1995 reform shows that Swedish fathers increased the amount of time taken by an average of fifteen days. (Swedish mothers still account for about 80 percent of the highly compensated leave days.) Although it is rumored that the fathers' periods of leave tend to coincide with the Winter Olympics and other major sporting events, this is not borne out empirically. Fathers did take more leave when their children were between one and two years of age. And when the children were older than two years of age, there was a clear tendency among fathers to take parental leaves in the summer months and during Christmas, suggesting the use of leaves to prolong regular paid holidays. (The days of leave can be taken any time until the child reaches the age of eight.) As anticipated, Swedish fathers responded directly to the 1995 reform's "use it or lose it" incentive by using more days of leave. Still, the question remains about the extent to which this benefit-related shift spawns a more fundamental change in traditional gender roles. Indeed, when it came to the traditionally female task of caring for sick children, the researchers found no change in the fathers' share of care.[11]

In 2002 the Swedish system was reformed again as the government added 30 more days of parental leave compensated at 80 percent of the parent's salary, lifting the highly paid period of leave up to 390 days and bringing the total leave to 480 days. At the same time the government upped the ante, allocating 60 days of the total leave to fathers only—resulting in two daddy months. Further reforms were considered in 2005, including a proposal to expand the period of 80 percent compensation to fifteen months, with five months each reserved for the father and mother and allocation of the remaining five months left to the parents' discretion.[12]

As parental leave in Sweden presses on toward greater gender equality, public opinion lags somewhat behind the ambitions of policy makers and gender feminists. Although in principle gender equality and parental leave are widely supported, less than half the parents in both Sweden and the United States think that men and women should participate equally in paid employment and child care.[13] Swedish men still take only a small percentage of the leave to which they are entitled, and this leave tends to be concentrated among highly educated men in the public sector.[14]

In the United States, fathers are spending more time with their children and shouldering a greater share of household work today than in the past, even without highly compensated parental leave. Increased equality has loosened the shackles of traditional gender hierarchy in domestic relations and cleared the path for the transferring of women's labor from the household to the market—thus broadening women's horizons. Statutory provisions (such as child care and parental leave) emanating from the halls of Congress, along with organizational adjustments (such as flexible working hours) crafted on the ground floor of workplace settings, have expanded the opportunities for mothers to engage in paid employment. These various developments represent significant progress in the struggle to reconcile motherhood and labor-force participation. Certainly, much more remains to be done along these lines to balance the demands of work and family life for mothers who must work out of genuine necessity, who wish to pursue paid careers, or who are already the primary earner in their family (about one-third of all working wives earned more than their husbands in 2004).[15]

However, these two broad avenues for reconciling work and family life are essentially designed to carry traffic in one direction—the objective of both is to move mothers into paid employment while raising young children. The tenets of gender equality demand not only that men bear an equal share of domestic activity but that women keep up with men in the world of work. To do that, they have to start working as early as men. Public provisions of child care, family leave, and regulated work schedules make it possible (though not easy) to raise young children while maintaining an ongoing and relatively stable pattern of employment outside the home—a lifestyle preferred by many, though clearly not all, women. This approach follows what I have called the male model, which basically involves a seamless transition from school into the paid labor force along with a drive to rise as high as possible in a given line of work.

The male model remains the prevailing expectation among gender feminists. The pattern of an early start and a continuous work history imposes a temporal frame on policies to balance work and family life. Within this frame the idea of "balancing" refers to the concurrent performance of labor-force participation and childrearing activities. Just as policies promoting the male model deserve public support, so too, I would argue, do alternatives that offer aid and encouragement to women who want to follow a different course in life's journey through motherhood and employment. In posing these alternatives my objective is to sketch neither a comprehensive list of policy options nor an elaborate blueprint for a particular initiative. My purpose is to broaden public perceptions of the choices and help reframe the debate—a pursuit toward which efforts are already afoot.[16]

Having It All—One Step at a Time

At the start of family life when children need full-time care, the male model tends to narrow the perception of choices about the role of motherhood: either stay at home and invest in childrearing activities or compete with men on equal footing by entering the labor force early and staying for the long haul. From this perspective, the only way women can have both children and a career is by relying on day care and other family-friendly policies, and encouraging men to assume a larger share of cooking, cleaning, and caring. Having children, of course, does not automatically limit the opportunities of motherhood to two mutually exclusive options: remaining in the traditional role—barefoot, pregnant, and in the kitchen, as it is sometimes disparagingly depicted—or joining the fast track of professional life while outsourcing childrearing and domestic responsibilities. By taking a long view of motherhood over an expected lifetime of about eighty years (twenty years more than the life expectancy of mothers just a couple of generations earlier), we allow for the possibility that a "balance" between motherhood and employment might be achieved by sequential as well as simultaneous patterns of paid and domestic work. From this perspective, women who want to combine a life of motherhood and employment could have it all—one step at a time.

Mothers choosing to follow a sequential pattern, for example, might invest all their energies in child care and domestic activities for five to ten years and then spend the remainder of their active years in paid employment. The contributions of mothers to their families and to society vary according to different stages of the family life cycle. There are good reasons why some women would prefer to stay home during their children's preschool years. The early years of childhood are critical for social and cognitive development; some mothers want to invest more heavily in shaping this development than in advancing their employment prospects. Home care during the early childhood years is labor intensive, which heightens the economic value of the homemaker's contribution during that period. Then, after five or even ten years at home, women would still have more than thirty years to invest in paid employment—

enough time for most people to fully experience (perhaps even extinguish) the alleged joys of labor-force participation.

Clearly, the sequential pattern of mothers balancing work and family life is not to everyone's advantage. The cost would probably be too high for dual-earner families in which women are the primary earners. In other cases, investing five to ten years in child care and household management would derail careers from the fast track; for example, it would limit participation in occupations that require early training, many years of preparation, or the athletic prowess of youth. And a later start lessens the likelihood of rising to the very top of the corporate ladder. Those are the trade-offs for enjoying the choice of two callings in life.

As the world of work beckons to women, the domestic role of motherhood, especially in caring for young children, has become contested ground. Some women want to keep the responsibilities of childrearing entirely as their own, and others want to distribute a greater share of responsibility to men and public day-care authorities. The response to the tensions surrounding motherhood varies among different cultures. Affirming the domestic role of motherhood, Article 41 of the Irish Constitution recognizes "that by her life within the home, woman gives to the State a support without which the common good cannot be achieved. The State shall, therefore, endeavour to ensure that mothers shall not be obliged by economic necessity to engage in labour to the neglect of their duties in the home."[17] (The Irish Constitution also explicitly protects the rights of men and women who work outside the home.) During a parliamentary committee review of the Irish Constitution, charges that Article 41, particularly the gender emphasis, was flawed and outdated were met with a lyrical defense by the Mothers at Home organization:

Childcare's what they call it now, big business I
hearsay.
It's what our mammies did for years without a
thought of pay.
But what about the mammies who want to stay at
home?
Must they be now forced out to work and leave
their care alone!

It's right for those who want to go. They're quite
entitled to.
But what of those who want to stay? What are
they supposed to do?
We're only small for just a time. Our childhood
will pass by
Without our mums to care for us. It's enough to
make us cry!

A Nation's wealth is measured by more than
stocks and shares.
It's by how we treat each other—how we have
loved and cared.
The mothers of this Nation are doing a mighty
deed,
Now the children of the country are very much in
need. . . .[18]

The Irish appreciation of motherhood has not kept women from working outside the home. In 2004 the labor-force participation of Irish women, though not as high as in the Nordic countries, was less than 1 percent below the average for the fifteen original European Union countries. Between 1991 and

2004 female employment rates in Ireland registered the highest growth among the thirty member nations of the OECD.[19] The Irish Constitution's recognition of motherhood, along with a limited tax credit of approximately 770 Euros (about $1,000) available to mothers and fathers for home care of dependents, affords greater public respect and value to the role in Ireland than we find in the United States.

Although most mothers have some choice in determining how to balance work and family, the cultural context in the United States, along with much of the advanced industrial world, favors the male model of early entry and continuous labor-force participation rather than the sequential approach. In addition, as we have seen, the capitalist ethos underrates the economic value and social utility of domestic labor in family life, particularly during the early years of childhood; the prevailing expectations of gender feminists place too high a value on the social and psychological satisfactions of work; and the typical package of family-friendly benefits delivered by the state creates incentives that essentially reinforce the devaluations of motherhood prompted by the capitalist ethos and feminist expectations.

Is there a way to reshape these influential forces to correct the social imbalance currently encountered by mothers trying to decide how to reconcile work and family life? It is hard to see how the capitalist ethos can be moderated, short of an almost spiritual conversion in public attitudes that rebuffs material consumption and the commodification of everyday life. I detect no such change on the horizon. Yet, just as the capitalist knack for creative destruction has contributed to the outsourcing of family household production, it is possible that the innovative genius of the free market might create in-home work for millions of people. If my phone request for computer service can be patched out to a worker somewhere in India, why not directly into the residences of stay-at-home workers in the United States? The information-technology revolution may yet spawn a renewal of family life and home parenting as people increasingly shop from home and commute electronically to work.[20]

Feminist expectations are another matter. There are some signs that the emerging generation of leaders among college-educated women are beginning to question how well the male model suits their ambitions in life. They may no longer be satisfied with the trade-offs inherent in earlier expectations. A 2006 *Newsweek* article on the next generation of women leaders claims that lately the talk among work-family advocates has changed. Rather than trying to persuade women to stay on track toward leadership positions, according to Daniel McGinn, the new discourse is "focused on finding ways to support women's 'non-linear' career paths—and to build better 'on ramps' for women wishing to return to work after career pauses."[21] He notes an increasing number of high-profile role models who are taking time off from their careers, including the actress Calista Flockhart, who is returning to television after spending five years at home with her child. Further indications of change are registered in national surveys, which reveal an increasing lack of enthusiasm for full-time work outside the home. From 1997 to 2007 the percentage of both employed and at-home mothers who considered full-time work to be their ideal situation declined by one-third.[22] The extent to which feminist expectations may shift is ultimately an issue that women will decide for themselves.

Finally, there is the role of the state and the question of how to deliver family-friendly policies that provide an equitable set of work-family incentives, benefiting both those who value an early start on paid employment and those who prefer to invest more time in childrearing and domestic life.

Balancing the Ledger of Family Policy

The customary package of family-friendly policies provides the kind of benefits that transmit both public support for and confirmation of the life choices of mothers with young children who opt for the male model of early entry and continuous labor-force participation. At the same time, the state offers few, if any, benefits that aid and endorse mothers inclined toward the sequential approach to balancing work and family life. Neither the simultaneous nor the sequential approach to work and family life is so unmistakably superior in promoting private happiness and the public good that it deserves exclusive backing from the state. Something needs to be done to correct the current discrepancy in public incentives and symbolic approval, which skews the social context of modern lifestyle choices.

To propose that public officials rethink the conventional design of family-friendly policy is not to dispute the importance and value of subsidized day-care services, paid parental leave, sick leave for dependent care, and other measures that make it possible to manage the concurrent approach to work and family life in the early childrearing years. The objective here is not to reduce public subsidies for existing benefits but rather to increase flexibility and choice by extending family-friendly policies beyond the established realm of work-oriented supports.

Three goals frame various initiatives to balance the ledger of family policy by lending equal weight to the sequential approach to childrearing and paid employment. These goals involve recognizing the economic worth of motherhood, particularly during the preschool years; facilitating the transition of women's labor from the household to the market after the early years of childrearing; and protecting against the heightened insecurity faced by mothers who elect to care for their children at home.

Arguably the most essential way to acknowledge the economic value of motherhood is the same way we recognize the worth of all caring services in society—that is, to pay for it. In 2000 the federal government provided about $16 billion to subsidize a variety of cash and in-kind benefits for working parents who placed their children in day care, and such public spending is on the rise. In addition, a few states have started to provide universal preschool programs, and others are taking the provision of universal preschool under consideration. No equivalent public support is offered to parents caring for their own children at home.

A home-care allowance to full-time homemakers with children up to five years of age would afford mothers greater freedom to choose between caring for their own children and placing them in state-subsidized day care. (Of course, if the provision of a home-care allowance ever came to pass, it should be made available to either parent. It is evident, however, that this benefit—as with Swedish parental leave—would be drawn on mostly by mothers.) Although it is generally naive to assume that social benefits can be expanded in one realm of family policy without constricting the availability of support in other areas, this is not necessarily the case when the objective is to provide choice. Under a publicly subsidized system of universal day care, for example, the state could actually reduce expenditures by giving mothers the choice between consuming the public day-care service for which their child is eligible and receiving a cash grant for home care, calculated at 80 percent of the cost of the subsidized service.

Various objections to such a measure would no doubt ask: What about welfare mothers? And rich mothers? And gender equality? Regarding welfare mothers and rich mothers, some constraints would have to be set. To guard against home-care benefits that would end up disproportionately subsidizing wealthy families, these schemes could be progressively indexed as a refundable tax credit that tapers off rapidly for those earning more than twice the median family income. In addition, it could be limited to cover the first five years of care for up to three children. This would create a time-limited benefit that is longer than the period of welfare coverage currently available under the Temporary Assistance for Needy Families program, but not as open-ended as the social assistance benefits previously available in the Aid to Families with Dependent Children program. Although the home-care allowance might create some incentive for low-income mothers to stay at home during the early years of childrearing, it is not necessarily the case that on balance such an outcome would be harmful to their children or society. (In any case, few if any social policies dealing with family life have no negative side effects.)

As for the issue of gender equality, feminist arguments that allowing mothers to choose between a simultaneous and sequential approach to work and family life is detrimental to women's interests rest on a wholeheartedly authoritarian claim that what is advantageous for some women, particularly those in the elite professional classes, is best for all women. This argument advances the position that caring for children is a job the government should pay for only when it is performed by strangers, most of whom are women. Publicly subsidized day care, whether in the form of collective arrangements in day-care centers or nannies in individual homes, tends to redistribute the role of mothering. Women best qualified to command high salaries in the marketplace delegate the responsibility to others with less marketable potential. (Some men certainly might enter this work and do it as well as, if not better than, some women. But honestly, how many readers would be comfortable dropping off their three-year-old daughter in a day-care center staffed by three forty-year-old men whose marketable skills did not commend them to more gainful activities?)

A home-care allowance would probably lead to more mothers staying at home with their children for longer periods of time than at present. This would not mean a return to traditional family life as it was practiced half a century ago. Whatever changes a home-care allowance might bring, birth control technology, market forces, civil rights legislation, and modern sensibilities seem to assure that there is no turning back the clock on gender relations. In this regard, I should repeat for the sake of emphasis that all the measures being discussed here—home-care allowances, social credits, and other benefits—to balance the public incentives of family policy should apply with equal consequence to both mothers and fathers who might elect to provide home care for their children. Moreover, these measures should be flexible, so that parents who so wished could share the benefits by alternating periods in which each assumed the full-time homemaking responsibilities. I would fully expect that in some cases, particularly in families where the mothers were the primary earners, the benefits would be drawn upon mainly by stay-at-home fathers. I discuss these benefits in terms of their use by mothers, however, because of the reality that more often than not mothers would be the ones choosing to invest in the endeavors of childrearing and domestic life.

The proposal for a home-care allowance is neither unique nor revolutionary. Many countries provide a cash allowance for home care for the elderly which can be used to pay relatives.[23] And for decades in the United States, feminist organizers, politicians, religious leaders, and academics have backed the development of policies supporting in-home child care.[24] In the 1920s, feminists in the mothers' pensions movement sought financial aid that was initially described as a childrearing salary, which "inevitably raised the possibility of paying all mothers."[25] In 1980 the White House Conference on Families recommended that homemaking be classified as a career, and that tax credits be established for full-time homemakers. These recommendations, however, were buried far down in the list of more than 150 recommendations adopted by the delegates.[26] A few years later, in 1983, the Vatican published a "Charter on the Rights of the Family," which counseled that social measures such as remuneration for work in the home should be taken so that "mothers will not be obliged to work outside the home to the detriment of family life and especially of the education of the children."[27] And in the 1990s various groups proposed the reform of U.S. tax policy to make parents who stayed home to care for their preschool children eligible for the child-care tax credit.[28] Despite these encouragements, proposals for home-care benefits have not gained much purchase on the modern agenda of U.S. advocates of family-friendly policy. Instead, public discourse tends to focus on nonmaternal care, parental leave, men assuming more household duties, and other arrangements that support the simultaneous performance of paid work and childrearing responsibilities.[29]

In Europe, by contrast, home-care policy has sparked public debate and significant division in the measures taken by governments.[30] Indeed, home-care benefits are the centerpiece of the "neofamilialist" model, which is seen as one of the dominant European child-care alternatives. Offering long-term payments for in-home care (three to four years per child), the new familialism emphasizes a woman's right to choose between a housewife-mother role and labor-force participation in the childrearing years, rather than simply choosing from among different types of nonmaternal care. This approach to family policy is followed in Norway, Finland, France, Belgium, and Austria. An alternative approach adheres to the egalitarian model of Denmark and Sweden, which emphasizes the provision of universal nonparental care services and the equal division of remaining child-care and domestic responsibilities between fathers and mothers.

Although family-friendly policies of the Nordic countries are often spoken of in one breath, on the matter of a woman's right to spend a significant period as a stay-at-home mother there is a clear division, with Sweden and Denmark on the one side and Norway and Finland on the other.[31] When most advocates of family-friendly policies in the United States recommend emulating the Nordic model, they are *not* referring to the decisive lifestyle choices advanced by the essential home-care policies of Finland and Norway.

In 1998, Norway initiated a policy to pay cash benefits to all families with children up to three years old who were not enrolled in a state-subsidized day-care center. According to the Norwegian Ministry of Children and Family Affairs, this policy was designed to permit parents to spend more time caring for their own children and to give them genuine freedom of choice regarding child-care arrangements. It also sought to introduce greater equality in the cash transfers that parents received from the state—regardless of child-care arrangements. In 2004, home-care payments amounted to approximately $595 per month, at which time 70 percent of the children under three years old were cared for at home.[32] Finland employs a similar policy, which was fully implemented in 1989. Between 1989 and 1995, labor-force participation among Finnish women with children under three years old declined from 68 to 55 percent.[33] In 2005 approximately 70 percent of Finnish children between one and two years old were cared for by their parents, who received support from home-care and parental-leave benefits. In 2002 Austria implemented a new home-care benefit that provides approximately $570 per month to parents of children who are under four years old—along with social security pension, health insurance, and accident insurance. France has a complex system of family benefits that includes a parental education and upbringing allowance for home care until the child is three years old.

Home-care benefits facilitate the childrearing phase of a sequential approach to work and family life, which might last from five to ten years depending on the number of children in the family. Although the lifelong job of motherhood is far from over when children enter grade school, the full-time demands of daily care are greatly reduced—along with the caregiver's economic contribution to family life. At this juncture, women who chose to be stay-at-home mothers during the early childhood years encounter the challenge of shifting their labor from the home to the market. With a large gap in their résumés, they are somewhat disadvantaged in the search for work compared to women who follow the male model of early entry and continuous employment. Still, one might argue that for many jobs prospective employers should judge reentry mothers as more attractive candidates than younger women fresh out of school. Having gone through the critical junctures of childbearing, early child care, marriage (usually), and sometimes even divorce, reentry mothers are likely to be more mature and stable workers than younger women for whom the future remains uncertain. Admittedly, however, this view has not yet captured the popular imagination of human-resource personnel.[34] Thus, to balance the ledger of family policy, home-care benefits need to be supplemented with policies that smooth the transition into paid employment.

Transitional policies have already been established in several countries. France, for example, introduced a measure in 2000—the Return-to-Work Incentive for Women—which offers a temporary cash benefit to stay-at-home mothers who cared for at least one child under the age of six when they return to a job, start a business, or enter a training program.[35] Similarly, Australia provides a return-to-work credit of $1,200 for education and training for parents who spend two years caring full-time for their children.[36] An alternative policy might involve a "social credit" awarded by the government for each year spent at home with up to three children under the age of five.[37] When the mother is ready to enter or reenter the labor market, the accumulated credits could be exchanged for various benefits that would assist her in making the transition. For example, the credits could be applied to cover tuition for academic training and enrollment in technical schools, or they might be traded for preferential points on federal civil-service examinations. As with the home-care benefit, concerns about the social credits unfairly benefiting the wealthy could be allayed by setting an appropriate family-income limit for eligibility. The social credit scheme would be somewhat akin to veterans' benefits, which were granted in recognition of people who sacrificed career opportunities while serving the nation. Homemakers sacrifice employment opportunities to invest their energies in shaping the moral and physical stock of future citizens. By recognizing this contribution to national well-being, the social credit scheme would revive the sagging status of motherhood.

Even with a home-care allowance and transitional policies, postponing entry into the labor force is a risky proposition for young mothers. Among other concerns, the modern probability of divorce, volatility of the marketplace, the erosion of health-insurance coverage, and dire predictions about the future of social security pensions pose an uncomfortable bundle of vulnerabilities for the stay-at-home mother. What happens to the family's health insurance if her husband loses his job? How will she fare in old age without paying into social security during the childrearing years? What resources will she be left with in the event of a divorce? There are no guarantees against the vicissitudes of modern times. To lend equal draw to the sequential approach to work and family life, however, the final entries on the ledger of family policy should offer a measure of protection against the risks accentuated by withdrawal from the labor force for a period of childrearing.

Although home-care allowances afford some immediate compensation for childrearing, these benefits do not insure against illness or the inevitable decline of income in old age. In the United States, the prevalence of employment-related health insurance is a powerful motivator for early entry and continuous participation in the labor market. Although most middle-class stay-at-home mothers would be covered under their spouses' health-insurance plans, the risk of divorce and unemployment, along with the absence of insurance coverage in low-wage occupations, poses a level of insecurity surrounding access to health care, which would drive many women away from the opportunity of home-care. Access to health care is, of course, a complex and pressing issue that goes well beyond the matter of balancing work and family life. In this context, though, it's worth noting that an arrangement for some form of universal health insurance would do much to allay the anxieties of young mothers contemplating a temporary retreat from the labor market.

As for worries about the decline of income in old age, mothers who stay home to care for their children lose the credits toward public pension benefits that would otherwise accrue if they were employed during that period. To offset this loss, several countries, including Austria, Sweden, Britain, and France, assign varying amounts of pension credit for caregiving. Sweden awards credit to either spouse for each year they care for a child under 3. In Britain people who interrupt careers to assume caregiving duties are compensated through the Home Responsibility Protection policy, which credits both men and women with a minimum level of contribution during the years they spend caring for their children or disabled family members.[38]

Yet, even with contribution credits added in for the time at home, at the end of the day women who temporarily leave work are still likely to qualify for pensions that are much lower than those earned by their husbands (or ex-husbands, as the case may be). Family-friendly policies designed to promote choice encourage fathers and mothers to divide up the work of paid employment and domestic labor according to their talents and personal inclinations, in order to further the mutual objectives of family life. After having made these decisions, it would seem only fair that parents be able to share equally in the assets and material benefits accrued by both parties to the family enterprise. In the case of pension entitlements this translates into policies such as those enacted in Canada and Germany, which dictate the splitting of benefit credits between spouses. The Canadian policy requires splitting only entitlements to public pensions, whereas the German scheme is broader in scope, encompassing all entitlements acquired in both public and private pensions. While spouses have legal rights to an equal share of their combined pension credits, in both of these countries the tangible division of old-age pension entitlements occurs only in cases of divorce.[39] Of course, the actual sharing of pensions need not be contingent upon divorce. One can imagine a credit-sharing arrangement based on a system of joint accounts that combine both partners' pension credits and issue checks for equal amounts to each party—conferring explicit recognition of each member's contribution to the family enterprise.

Unfortunately, those who advocate credit-sharing arrangements are currently swimming upstream. There is far from universal support for the view of married life as a partnership in which the members decide how to divide their labor to most efficiently satisfy their personal needs and family responsibilities, and share equally in the economic assets built up over time. For example, a 1991 report by the OECD Group of Experts on Women and Structural Change recommended that the individual, rather than the married couple, should be considered as the unit of entitlement for social security benefits in order to promote the wife's personal autonomy and economic independence.[40] Indeed, the avenue to gender equality is generally considered to be paved with the individualization of social rights. To move in this direction, the president of the Women's University in Belgium counsels "suppressing for able-bodied adults all the rights based on relations of marriage or cohabitation with an insuree."[41]

Over the years various groups in the United States have expressed serious interest in credit-sharing arrangements. In

1977 the National Women's Conference called for federal and state legislatures to base laws relating to property, inheritance, and domestic relations "on the principle that marriage is a partnership in which the contribution of each spouse is of equal importance and value."[42] Embracing this principle, the 1979 Advisory Council on Social Security recommended consideration of a credit-sharing scheme, but the proposal was stifled by entrenched interests. It reappeared in the early 1990s but did not gain political momentum.

Once we broach the subject of equal shares in social security pensions, it is a short step to applying the same principles of equality and security to other material resources acquired by both partners, regardless of who holds title to the property. In Germany, as noted, the scheme to split credits between spouses applies to all entitlements in both public and private pensions. In the United States, nine states have enacted community property laws that treat husbands and wives as partners in married life, each of whom is entitled to one-half interest in all employment income received (including private pension benefits) during marriage and all property acquired through such income. This exemplary policy not only imparts symbolic recognition to the egalitarian ideal of family life but also affords some protection against the loss of personal resources that young mothers risk by withdrawing their labor from the marketplace to invest in childrearing and household management.

Since the turn of the century, politicians on both sides of the aisle have been bidding for ownership of family values. As pressures build to help parents manage the contemporary challenges of work and childrearing, those looking to craft a pro-family agenda in the United States are likely to begin by fiddling with the standard package of family-friendly benefits—

nonmaternal day care and limited periods of paid parental leave. It is what they know best and hear most about from family-policy advocates. I put forth the case for rethinking the conventional approach neither to diminish efforts in this direction nor to cast doubt on their value to the many mothers who struggle with the daily demands of raising children and going to the office. My objective instead is to broaden the pro-family agenda by giving equal consideration to alternative approaches to balancing work and family life.

On several occasions I've been asked by women in professional life whether providing support for home care and the sequential pattern of mixing work and family life might detract from the status of mothers who work full-time and have young children in day care. It's a fair question that cuts both ways, as Ann Crittenden found out. After resigning from a high-profile job at the *New York Times* to stay home with her infant son, she ran into an acquaintance who asked, "Didn't you used to be Ann Crittenden?"[43] As things now stand, the predominant policy proposals are far from neutral in offering incentives that lend public approval and economic support for early entry and continuous participation in the paid labor force along with the outsourcing of many traditional duties of motherhood. A home-care allowance reinforced by measures that would guarantee a basic level of health care, reform social security to incorporate credit-sharing, and extend the legal mandates of community property to all states in the union would do much to balance the ledger of family-friendly initiatives—and restore a sense of social admiration for motherhood.

Appendix: Data on Factors Related to Fertility

All of the data in this appendix refer to the discussion of relations between female employment, family policy, and fertility in Chapter 5. The data in Figure 1 show a negative relationship of $r = -.734$. Because we cannot assume that the data in these analyses (average rates of the same group of countries at different time periods) involve independent observations, Pearson's r cannot be used to test hypotheses or predict future relationships. It is reported here and elsewhere in this section only as a way to summarize the observed relationship between two variables.

Depending which countries and time frame are being analyzed, one can find different patterns. For example, based on the data available for the fifteen original member countries of the European Union, we see in Figures 2 and 3 that a negative relationship between fertility and female employment rates ($r = -.545$) is clearly evident between 1994 and 1998, and that a positive relationship appears ($r = .763$) between 1999 and 2004. Still, in 2004 the average fertility rate is far below replacement and below that in 1980. The data in Figure 4 have a negative relationship of $r = -.809$.

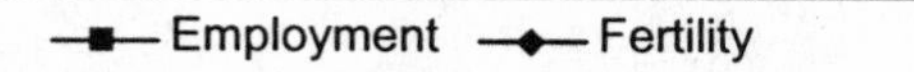

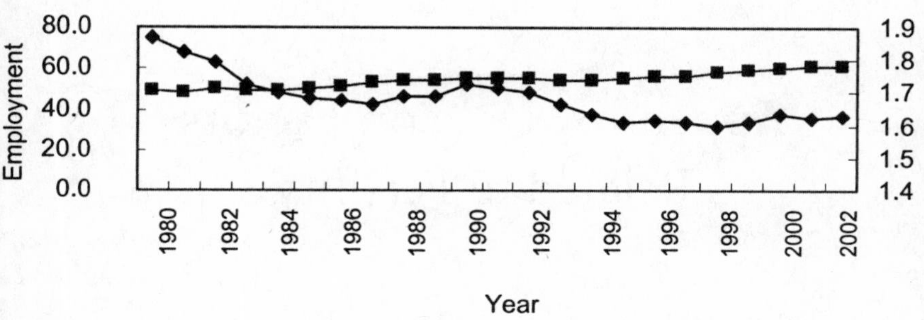

Figure 1. Average female employment rates and fertility rates among seventeen OECD countries, 1980–2002. Data are from OECD, *Society at a Glance: OECD Social Indicators, 2005*, http://www.oecd.org/document/24/0,2340,en_2825_497118_2671576_1_1_1_1,00.html.

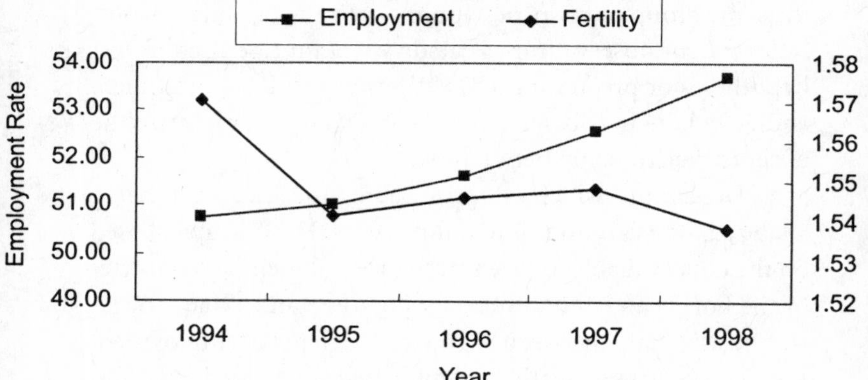

Figure 2. Average female employment rates and fertility rates among fifteen EU countries, 1994–1998. Data are from the Eurostat database, http://epp.eurostat.ec.europa.eu.

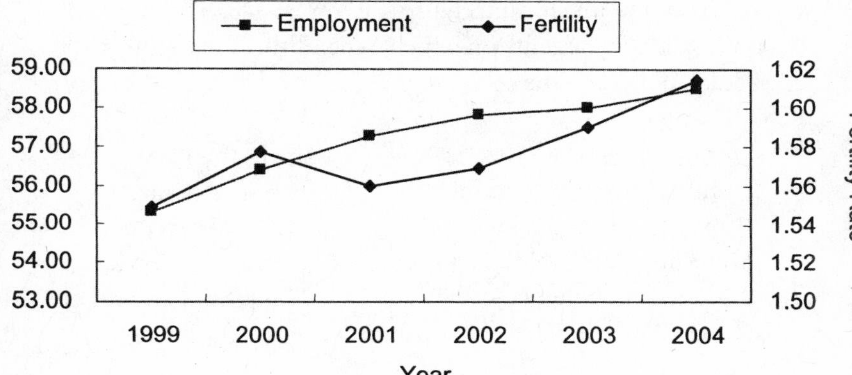

Figure 3. Average female employment rates and fertility rates among fifteen EU countries, 1999–2004. Data are from the Eurostat database, http://epp.eurostat.ec.europa.eu.

Figure 4. Average female employment rates and marriage rates among fifteen OECD countries, 1980–2002. Data are from OECD, *Society at a Glance: OECD Social Indicators, 2005*, http://www.oecd.org/document/24/0,2340, en_2825_497118_2671576_1_1_1_1,00.html.

The relationship in Figure 5 is $r = -.386$. The range of family-friendly benefits on which expenditures in Figure 5 are calculated include the following:

FAMILY CASH BENEFITS	FAMILY SERVICES
Family allowances for children	Family day care
Family support benefits	Personal services
Maternity and parental leave	Household services
Lone-parent benefits	Household and other in-kind benefits
Other cash benefits	

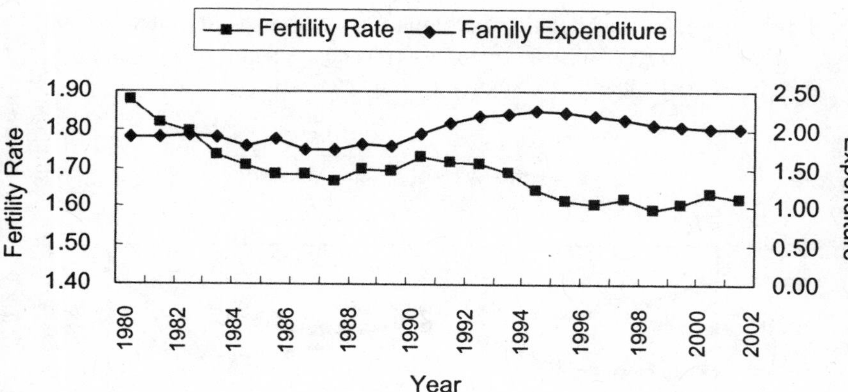

Figure 5. Average fertility rates and family-friendly expenditure as percentage of GDP among seventeen OECD countries, 1980–2002. Total fertility rates are from OECD, *Society at a Glance: OECD Social Indicators, 2005*, http://www.oecd.org/document/24/0,2340,en_2649_201185_2671576_1_1_1_1,00.html; family-friendly expenditure data are from OECD, *Social Expenditure Database (SOCX, 2004), 1980–2001*, http://www.oecd.org/document/2/0,2340,en_2649_201185_31612994_1_1_1_1,00.html.

The correlation between fertility and total expenditure in Figure 6 is $r = -.655$. Based on earlier calculations for fifteen European Union countries the relationship between social expenditures and marriage was $r = -.788$ (from Neil Gilbert, "Conservative Lifestyle Choices: Preference, Class, and Social Policy," paper presented at the Institute on Culture, Religion, and World Affairs Conference on Women and Conservatism in America, Boston University, May 2004).

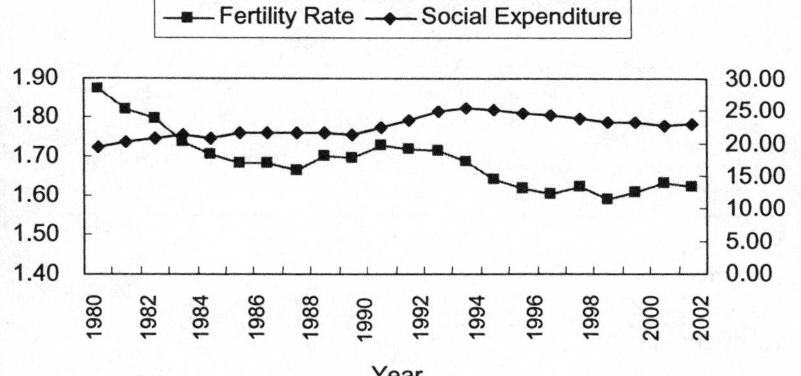

Figure 6. Average fertility rates and total social expenditure as percentage of GDP among seventeen OECD countries, 1980–2002. Total fertility rates are from OECD, *Society at a Glance: OECD Social Indicators, 2005*, http://www.oecd.org/document/24/0,2340,en_2649_201185_2671576_1_1_1_1,00.html; public expenditure data are from OECD, *Social Expenditure Database (SOCX, 2004), 1980–2001*, http://www.oecd.org/document/2/0,2340,en_2649_201185_31612994_1_1_1_1,00.html.

Table 1. Difference in Fertility Rates and Female Labor-Force Participation, 1994–2004

	Fertility rates	Female labor-force participation
Sweden	−0.13	+2.0
Finland	−0.05	+6.9
Denmark	−0.03	+4.7

Source: OECD, *Society at a Glance: OECD Social Indicator, 2005*. http://www.oecd.org/document/24/0,2340,en_2649_201185_2671576_1_1_1_1,00.html.

Table 2. Comparison of Religious Values in Europe and the United States, 1990–1991

	Percentage who rated the importance of God in their lives as "10" on a 10-point scale	Percentage who attend religious services at least once a month
Belgium	13	35
Finland	12	13
France	10	17
East Germany	13	20
West Germany	14	33
Great Britain	16	25
Iceland	17	9
Ireland	40	88
Italy	29	47
Netherlands	11	31
Norway	15	13
Spain	18	40
Sweden	8	10
Switzerland	26	43
European Average	17.3	30.3
United States	48	59

Source: Ronald Inglehart and Wayne Baker, "Modernization, Cultural Change, and the Persistence of Cultural Values," *American Sociological Review* 65 (February 2000), tables 6 and 7.

Notes

Introduction

1. Stephanie Coontz, *Marriage, a History: How Love Conquered Marriage* (New York: Penguin Books, 2005).

2. See *Eisenstadt v. Baird* (405 U.S. 438). The distribution of contraceptives to minors was legalized in 1977 in the case of *Carey v. Population Services International* (431 U.S. 678).

3. For a lively exchange on this issue see David Popenoe, "American Family Decline, 1960–1990: A Review and Appraisal"; Norval Glenn, "A Plea for Objective Assessment of Family Decline"; Judith Stacey, "Good Riddance to 'The Family': A Response to David Popenoe"; Philip Cowan, "The Sky Is Falling, but Popenoe's Analysis Won't Help Us Do Anything about It"; David Popenoe, "The National Family Wars," all in the *Journal of Marriage and the Family* 55, no. 3 (August 1993), 525–553.

4. Paula Foss, "The Past Is Not a Foreign Country: The Historical Education of Policy," in Jill Berrick and Neil Gilbert, eds., *Raising Children: Emerging Needs, Modern Risks, and Social Responses* (New York: Oxford University Press 2008).

Chapter 1. The Social Context

1. The monthly ADC grants of $18 for the first child and $12 for each additional child were based roughly on the amount received by families of soldiers who lost their lives in World War I. James Leiby, *History of Social Welfare and Social Work in the United States* (New York: Columbia University Press, 1978).

2. For a detailed review of these developments see Neil Gilbert, "Welfare Policy in the U.S.: The Road from Income Maintenance to Workfare," in Neil Gilbert and Antoine Parent, eds., *Welfare Reform: A Comparative Assessment of French and U.S. Experiences* (New Brunswick, N.J.: Transaction, 2003).

3. Sylvia Ann Hewlett, *Creating a Life: Professional Women and the Quest for Children* (New York: Miramax Books, 2002).

4. Garance Franke-Ruta, "Creating a Lie: Sylvia Ann Hewlett and the Myth of the Baby Bust," *American Prospect*, July 1, 2002, 31.

5. Ibid., 33.

6. Janice Horowitz, Julie Rawe, and Sora Song, "Making Time for a Baby," *Time*, April 15, 2002, 48–54.

7. Lisa Belkin, "The Opt-Out Revolution," *New York Times Magazine*, October 26, 2003.

8. See, for example, Bee Lavender, "Revolution or Regression," November 17, 2003, http://www.hipmama.com/?q=node/view/357; Katie Granju, "Against Opting Out: Just Guessing, but They May Want Back In," December 23, 2003, http://www.ifeminists.net/introduction/editorials/2003/1223granju.html.

9. Tatsha Robertson, "Stay-at-Home 'Mommy Set' Seen as Latest Privileged Class," *Boston Globe*, December 19, 2004.

10. Claudia Wallis, "The Case for Staying Home: Why More Young Moms Are Opting Out of the Rat Race," *Time*, March 22, 2004, 51–59.

11. David Brooks, "The Year of Domesticity," *New York Times*, January 1, 2006.

12. Joan Williams, "The Opt-Out Revolution Revisited," *American Prospect*, March 5, 2007. For the full report on which this story was based see Joan Williams, Jessica Manvell, and Stephanie Bornstein, "'Opt Out' or Pushed Out? How the Press Covers Work/Family Conflict," Center for WorkLife Law, Hastings College of the Law, University of California, San Francisco, 2006.

13. The Institute for American Values is a small think tank that punches well above its weight in media coverage. See, for example, Martha Farrell Erickson and Enola Aird, *The Motherhood Study: Fresh Insights on Mothers' Attitudes and Concerns* (New York: Institute for American Values, 2005); Linda Matchan, "Lawyer Finds New Life Waiting at Home," *Boston Globe*, February 20, 2003; Carol Mithers, "Changemaker," *Ladies Home Journal*, May 2003, 98–99; Sue Shellenbarger, "Women's Groups Give Peace a Chance in War of At-Home and Working Moms," *Wall Street Journal*, December 12, 2002.

14. Enola Aird, "On Rekindling a Spirit of 'Home Training': A Mother's Notes from the Front," in Sylvia Ann Hewlett, Nancy Rankin, and Cornell West, *Taking Parenting Public: The Case for a New Social Movement* (Lanham, Md.: Rowman and Littlefield, 2002).

15. Maureen Dowd, "What's a Modern Girl to Do?" *New York Times*, October 30, 2005.

16. Belkin, "Opt-Out Revolution."

17. Claudia Goldin, "The Quiet Revolution That Transformed Women's Employment, Education and Family," 2006 Ely Lecture, American Economic Association Meetings, Boston, Mass., January 2006.

18. Ibid.

19. Katherine Bradbury and Jane Katz, "Women's Rise: A Work in Progress," *Federal Reserve Bank of Boston Regional Review* 14, no. 3 (2005), 58–67.

20. Ibid.

21. Ibid. Analyzing the data from the Bureau of Labor Statistics monthly surveys, Bradbury and Katz found no decline in women's earnings. There was, however, a slowdown in real wage growth for women, which was less than 12 percent between 1994 and 2004, compared to a 19 percent rise in earnings between 1983 and 1993.

22. Ibid. The authors found no evidence of a shift in attitudes and norms of working men and women in data from surveys conducted by the Families and Work Institute, but they allow that a normative change "might not be captured in these questions because of the way they are worded" (67).

23. Julie Hotchkiss, "What's Up with the Decline in Female Labor Force Participation?" Federal Reserve Bank of Atlanta Working Paper, no. 2005-18, August 2005.

24. Neil Gilbert, *Welfare Justice: Restoring Social Equity* (New Haven: Yale University Press, 1995).

25. Anthony Trollope, "The Lady of Launay," in *Why Frau Frohmann Raised Her Prices and Other Stories* (London: Penguin Books, 1993, first published in 1882), 145. In the end, the Lady of Launay relented and allowed Bessy and Philip to marry—not because she reassessed the value of happiness but because they simply refused to bend to her will.

26. A 2001 poll conducted for *American Demographics* magazine found that among girls ages thirteen to twenty, 56 percent agreed with the statement "A man should always open the door for a woman," 35 percent had no opinion, and only 8 percent disagreed. Cited in Karlyn Bowman, "Women and Conservatism: AEI Studies in Public Opinion," paper presented at the Conference on Women and Conservatism in America, Institute on Culture, Religion and World Affairs, Boston University, May 8–9, 2004.

27. Claudia Goldin and Maria Shim, "Making a Name: Women's Surnames at Marriage and Beyond," *Journal of Economic Perspectives* 18, no. 2 (Spring 2004), 143–160.

28. Bradbury and Katz, "Women's Rise."

29. Barbara Dafoe Whitehead and David Popenoe, *The State of Our Unions 2002* (Piscataway, N.J.: The National Marriage Project, 2002), 26.

30. Paul Ehrlich, *The Population Bomb* (New York: Ballantine Books, 1968).

31. Heather Boushey, "Are Women Opting Out? Debunking the Myth," Center for Economic and Policy Research, Washington, D.C., November 2005.

32. U.S. Census Bureau, *Statistical Abstract of the United States: 2000* (Washington, D.C.: Government Printing Office, 2000), 195–196; U.S. Census Bureau, *Statistical Abstract of the United States: 2006* (Washington, D.C.: Government Printing Office, 2006).

33. U.S. Census Bureau, *Women Owned Firms 2002*, January 2006.

34. U.S. Department of Labor, Bureau of Labor Statistics, *Current Population Survey: 1988–2005 Annual Social and Economic Supplements*, 2005.

35. See Barbara Downs, "Fertility Rate of American Women: June 2002," in U.S. Census Bureau, *Current Population Reports (Oct. 2003)*, table 2.

36. Andrew Hacker, "The Case against Kids," *New York Review of Books*, November 30, 2000.

37. For a discussion of these other repercussions of the demographic shift, see Barbara Dafoe Whitehead, *The State of Our Unions 2006* (Piscataway, N.J.: National Marriage Project, 2006), 13–14.

38. Steve Sailer, "Baby Gap: How Birthrates Color the Electoral Map," *American Conservative*, December 20, 2004. Sailer points out that among the fifty states, plus Washington, D.C., the correlations between white total fertility and Bush's percentage of the vote were 0.85 in 2000 and 0.86 in 2004.

39. Phillip Longman, "The Return of Patriarchy," *Foreign Policy*, March–April 2006.

40. Ben Wattenberg, *The Birth Dearth: What Happens When People in Free Countries Don't Have Enough Babies?* (New York: Pharos Books, 1987).

41. See, for example, Catherine Hakim, *Work-Lifestyle Choices in the 21st Century* (Oxford: Oxford University Press, 2000); Daphne Spain and Suzanne Bianchi, *Balancing Act: Motherhood, Marriage, and Employment among American Women* (New York: Russell Sage Foundation, 1996); D. Coleman, "New Patterns and Trends in European Fertility: International and Sub-national Comparisons," in D. Coleman, ed., *Europe's Population in 1990* (Oxford: Oxford University Press, 1996).

42. Coleman, "New Patterns and Trends in European Fertility."

43. Jelle Visser, "The First Part-Time Economy in the World: A Model to be Followed?" *Journal of European Social Policy* 12, no. 1 (February 2002), 23–40.

44. T. Sobotka, "Is Lowest-Low Fertility in Europe Explained by the Postponement of Childbearing?" *Population and Development Review* 30, no. 2 (2004); Charlemagne, "The Fertility Bust," *Economist*, February 11, 2006, 50. Charlemagne suggests that the 1985 cohort of German women will experience a 30 percent rate of childlessness.

45. Eurostat, *Eurostat Yearbook 2002: The Statistical Guide to Europe* (Luxembourg: Office for Official Publications of the European Community, 2002).

46. In Norway we find a pattern of change in family size similar to that in the United States. Although the rate (12.3 percent) of women without children at age forty is smaller than in the United States, the cohort of Norwegian women at age forty in 1998 had a 25 percent higher rate of childlessness and a 35 percent higher rate of having one child than women at age forty in 1975. During the same period, Norwegian women with two children increased by 33 percent, and those with three or more children age forty declined by 33 percent. In 1998 Norwegian women at age forty with the most education had the highest rate of childlessness (19 percent). Trude Lappegard, "New Fertility Trends in Norway," *Demographic Research* 2, no. 3 (March 15, 2000), www.demographic-research.org/Volumes/Vol2/3. Hakim reports a somewhat higher rate of 14–15 percent of Norwegian women who are childless at age forty. Hakim, *Work-Lifestyle Choices*, 51.

47. U.S. Census Bureau, *Statistical Abstract of the United States: 2006*, 378.

48. Jeffrey Capizzano and Gina Adams, "The Hours That Children under Five Spend in Child Care: Variations across States," *New Federalism National Survey of American Families*, series B, no. B-8 (Washington, D.C.: Urban Institute, 2000).

49. Defamilialization is defined as "the degree to which households' welfare and caring responsibilities are relaxed either via welfare state provision or market pro-

vision." See Gosta Esping-Andersen, *Social Foundations of Postindustrial Economies* (Oxford: Oxford University Press, 1999), 51.

50. Fiona Williams, *Rethinking Families* (London: Calouste Gulbenkian Foundation, 2004).

51. Anthony Giddens, *The Transformation of Intimacy: Sexuality, Love, and Eroticism in Modern Society* (Cambridge, Eng.: Polity Press, 1992).

52. James Q. Wilson, "Why Not Just Live Together?" *American Experiment Quarterly* 4, no. 2 (Summer 2001), 30.

53. See *Griswold v. State of Connecticut* (381 U.S. 479).

54. Hakim, *Work-Lifestyle Choices.*

Chapter 2. Work and Family

1. Barbara Downs, "Fertility Rate of American Women: June 2002," in U.S. Census Bureau, *Current Population Reports (Oct. 2003),* table 2.

2. Expanding the frame to include marital status, sexual orientation, and income might generate additional categories. Weber's ideal types were not ideal in the sense of achieving perfection or representing exemplary values—they were meant as constructs that captured the central tendencies of a phenomenon. There were, as Weber put it, "ideal types of brothels as well as religions." See S. M. Miller, ed., *Max Weber: Selections from His Work* (New York: Thomas Crowell, 1963), 31.

3. Sharon Hays, *The Cultural Contradictions of Motherhood* (New Haven: Yale University Press, 1996).

4. Annette Lareau, *Unequal Childhoods: Class, Race, and Family Life* (Berkeley: University of California, 2003).

5. I would advise caution in forming generalizations from these studies, since both were based on rather small samples. Twelve families formed the core respondents in Lareau's sample—four middle class and eight working class or poor; Hays interviewed thirty-eight mothers—nineteen middle class and nineteen working class or poor.

6. For a more elaborate discussion of social partnerships and their implications, see Neil Gilbert, "Working Families: Hearth to Market," in Mary Ann Mason, Arlene Skolnick, and Stephen Sugarman, eds., *All Our Families: New Policies for a New Century* (New York: Oxford University Press, 2003).

7. Although there were high rates of childlessness during earlier periods of the twentieth century, the rates in 2002 were the highest ever for such prosperous and relatively peaceful times.

8. Citing the findings of the U.N.-supported World Fertility Survey in the 1970s, which revealed that primary infertility (inability to conceive or maintain a pregnancy) affects only 2–3 percent of women ages twenty-five to fifty, Hakim notes that infertility does not account for the sharp rise in childlessness after the mid-1970s. See Catherine Hakim, *Work-Lifestyle Choices in the 21st Century* (Oxford: Oxford University Press, 2000), 54.

9. Sylvia Ann Hewlett, *Creating a Life: Professional Women and the Quest for Children* (New York: Miramax Books, 2002); Claudia Goldin, "Career and Families: College Women Look to the Past," working paper no. 5188, National Bureau of Economic Research, Cambridge, Mass., July 1995.

10. Jan Walsh, *The Contrasexuals Report: A Report for Standard Life Bank in the Interests of Independent Minded and Adventurous Women!* (London: Standard Life Bank, October 2004).

11. Christine Dunn, "New Wave of Homebuyers: Single Women—After Married Couples, They Were the Top Homebuyers during 2005," *Providence Journal*, April 9, 2006.

12. Hewlett, *Creating a Life.*

13. Frank Newport, "Desire to Have Children Alive and Well in America," Gallup Poll Tuesday Briefing, August 19, 2003, http://www.galluppoll.com/content/?ci=9091&pg=1. Also see Goldin, "Career and Families," 33.

14. Amara Bachu, "Fertility of American Women: June 1992," in U.S. Census Bureau, *Current Population Reports,* no. P20-470 (Washington, D.C.: Government Printing Office, 1993).

15. Hays, *The Cultural Contradictions,* 109.

16. Gallup Organization, "American Families—1980," report submitted to the White House Conference on Families, June 5, 1980, by the Gallup Organization, Princeton, N.J.

17. Norval Glenn, "What the Numbers Say," *Family Affairs* 5, nos. 1–2 (1992), 5–7. Also see Barbara Defoe Whitehead and David Blankenhorn, "Man, Woman, and Public Policy: Difference and Dependency in the American Conversation" (New York: Institute for American Values, 1991).

18. Cited in Richard Wertheimer, Melissa Long, and Sharon Vandivere, "Welfare Recipients' Attitudes towards Welfare, Nonmarital Childbearing and Work: Implications for Reform," series B, no. B-37, Urban Institute, Washington, D.C., June 2001.

19. For a sample of the findings from these polls, see Family and Home Network, "Recent Surveys and Opinion Polls Regarding Work/Family Balance," http://www.familyandhome.org/media/Media_pr_surveys.htm.

20. W. Bradford Wilcox, response to critics of "What's Love Got to Do with It?" http://www.happiestwives.org/responsetocritics.htm; also see W. Bradford Wilcox and Steven Nock, "What's Love Got to Do with It?" *Social Forces,* March 2006.

21. Laura Kipnis, *Against Love: A Polemic* (New York: Vintage Books, 2003).

22. Hakim, *Work-Lifestyle,* 55.

23. For a reprinted copy of this Ann Landers column, originally published January 8, 1997, see members.aol.com/bren77065/page6.htm.

24. For example, see Elinor Burkett, *The Baby Boon: How Family Friendly America Cheats the Childless* (New York: Free Press, 2000).

25. Hakim, *Work-Lifestyle.*

26. Ronald Lee and Joshua Goldstein, "Rescaling the Life Cycle: Longevity and Proportionality," *Population and Development Review* 29 (2003), 183–207.

27. Goldin, "Career and Families."

28. Claudia Goldin, "The Quiet Revolution That Transformed Women's Employment, Education and Family," 2006 Ely Lecture, American Economic Association Meeting, Boston, Mass., January 2006.

29. T. J. Mathew and Brady E. Hamilton, "Mean Age of Mothers, 1970–2000," *National Vital Statistics Report,* 51, no. 1 (December 11, 2002).

30. Charlemagne, "The Fertility Bust," *Economist,* February 11, 2006, 50.

31. Lucy Kellaway, "Work-Life Imbalance," in *The World in 2007,* special issue, *Economist* (2006), 111.

Chapter 3. Capitalism and Motherhood

1. For a detailed analysis of this dynamic see Karl Marx, *Das Kapital,* edited by Friedrich Engels and condensed by Serge Levitsky (Chicago: Henry Regnery, 1959).

2. Joseph Schumpeter, *Capitalism, Socialism, and Democracy,* 3rd ed. (New York: Harper and Row, 1950; originally published in 1942), xiv.

3. The idea that the commercial achievements of capitalism sow the seeds of its own undoing was also advanced by Daniel Bell, who observed that the Protestant ethic was crushed by the invention of instant credit: credit cards enable immediate gratification, diminishing tendencies to plan and save. Daniel Bell, *The Cultural Contradictions of Capitalism* (New York: Basic Books, 1976), 21. Following this line of thought, Heilbroner declared that the commercial ethic of capitalism is depreciating its moral character. Robert Heilbroner, "The Demand for the Supply Side," *New York Review of Books,* June 11, 1981, 41.

4. Schumpeter, *Capitalism,* 409–425.

5. Ibid.

6. The virtues of capitalism are examined, for example, in James Q. Wilson, *The Moral Sense* (New York: Free Press, 1993), and David Marsland, "Markets and the Social Structure of Morality," *Society* 38, no. 2 (January–February 2001), 34–35.

7. See, for example, Jean Stefaniac and Richard Delgado, *No Mercy: How Conservative Think Tanks and Foundations Changed America's Social Agenda* (Philadelphia: Temple University Press, 1996); Robert Kuttner, "Philanthropy and Movements," *American Prospect* 13, no. 13 (July 15, 2002); Sally Covington, "Moving a Public Policy Agenda: The Strategic Philanthropy of Conservative Foundations," prepared for the National Committee for Responsive Philanthropy, Washington, D.C., 1995. Covington notes that a dozen conservative foundations, which controlled more than $1.1 billion in 1994, have funded a group of think tanks whose work "effectively repositioned the boundaries of national policy discussion, redefining key concepts, molding public opinion, and pushing for a variety of specific policy reforms."

8. Nathan Glazer, "Neoconservatives from the Start," *Public Interest,* Spring 2005.

9. For a more thorough examination of the evidence, see Neil Gilbert, *Transformation of the Welfare State: The Silent Surrender of Public Responsibility* (New York: Oxford University Press, 2002).

10. The social protection objective is sometimes said to assure the "decommodification" of labor by granting benefits that allow individuals and families to uphold a normal standard of living regardless of their performance in the labor market. For the most widely cited analysis of how decommodification is measured and applied to different countries, see Gosta Esping-Andersen, *The Three Worlds of Welfare Capitalism* (Princeton, N.J.: Princeton University Press, 1990). For a critical appraisal of the design and calculation of the decommodification index, see Rebecca Van Voorhis, "Different Types of Welfare States? A Methodological Deconstruction of Comparative Research," *Journal of Sociology and Social Welfare* 29, no. 4 (2002).

11. The initial use of profit-making organizations to deliver social welfare services in the United States is examined in Neil Gilbert, *Capitalism and the Welfare State* (New Haven: Yale University Press, 1983). The spread of privatization throughout the advanced industrial welfare states is analyzed in Neil Gilbert, *Transformation of the Welfare State.*

12. Mauricio Rojas, *Sweden after the Swedish Model: From Tutorial State to Enabling State* (Stockholm: Timbro, 2005), 67.

13. Barbara Kritzer, "Individual Accounts in Other Countries," *Social Security Bulletin* 66, no. 1 (2005), 32–36.

14. Information Office of the State Council of the People's Republic of China, White Paper on China's Employment Situation and Policies, 2004, www.china.org.cn/e-white/20040426.

15. According to Francis Fukuyama, free-market capitalism has triumphed to the point that the claims of many of its proponents have been stripped of all modesty. Fukuyama, *Trust: The Social Virtues and the Creation of Prosperity* (New York: Free Press, 1995).

16. Schumpeter, *Capitalism,* 161. The low birthrate in the 1930s was generally seen as a problem of survival, though not necessarily of the survival of capitalism per se. In Sweden, for example, Gunnar and Alva Myrdal were writing about the economic, social, and psychological effects of the declining birthrate. In response to the looming "population crisis," they recommended that the state promote family-friendly measures such as day care and parental leave. See Gunnar Myrdal, *Population: A Problem for Democracy* (Cambridge: Harvard University Press, 1940); Alva Myrdal, *Nation and Family* (New York: Harper, 1941).

17. According to this argument, Galbraith called for reduced private consumption and increased spending on public goods. See John K. Galbraith, *The Affluent Society* (New York: Mentor Books, 1958); Friedrich Hayek, "The Non Sequitur of the 'Dependence Effect,'" in Edmund Phelps, ed., *Private Wants and Public Needs* (New York: W. W. Norton, 1965), 37–43.

18. "Wedding Costs: For Poorer," *Economist,* June 14, 2003, 53.

19. During one of our urban hikes through Washington, D.C., Douglas Besharov treated me to the idea that these lavish affairs might represent an unconscious effort to compensate for the devalued social meaning of the event.

20. Inas Rashad and Michael Grossman, "The Economics of Obesity," *Public Interest* 156 (Summer 2004), 108.

21. Patricia M. Anderson, Kristin Butcher, and Philip Levine, "Maternal Employment and Overweight Children," *Journal of Health Economics* 22 (May 2003), 477–504.

22. Schumpeter, *Capitalism*, 83.

23. Debora Spar, *The Baby Business: How Money, Science and Politics Drive the Commerce of Conception* (Boston: Harvard Business School Press, 2006).

24. Irving Kristol, "Countercultures," *Commentary*, December 1944, 38.

25. Karl Marx and Friedrich Engels, "The Communist Manifesto," in Lewis Feuer, ed., *Marx and Engels: Basic Writings on Politics and Philosophy* (New York: Anchor Books, 1959), 25.

26. H. B. Mayo, *Democracy and Marxism* (New York: Oxford University Press, 1955), 234. Mayo describes the Bolshevik campaign against family life and other traditional ideas as a temporary episode.

27. Alan Carlson, "The Family, Public Policy and Democracy: Lessons from the Swedish Experiment," *The Family in America* 12, no. 8 (August 1998), 2

28. Schumpeter, *Capitalism*, 157.

29. Barry Schwartz, "Capitalism, the Market, the Underclass, and the Future," *Society* 37, no. 1 (November–December 1999), 40.

30. "No German Children? Then Pay Up," *Economist*, April 7–13, 2001, 54.

31. Schumpeter, *Capitalism*, 158.

32. Gary Becker, *A Treatise on the Family* (Cambridge: Harvard University Press, 1981).

33. There are also sources of sexually differentiated comparative advantages for both men and women outside of the reproductive process. But they can be highly provocative—as Harvard's ex-president Lawrence Summers can attest. For an informative and persuasive assessment of these differences, see Steven Pinker, *The Blank Slate: The Modern Denial of Human Nature* (New York: Penguin Books, 2002).

34. Ira Reiss, *Journey into Sexuality: An Exploratory Voyage* (Englewood Cliffs, N.J.: Prentice Hall, 1986).

35. S. B. Hrdy, *Mother Nature: A History of Mothers, Infants and Natural Selection* (New York: Pantheon Books, 1999); Judith Galtry, "Suckling and Silence in the USA: The Costs and Benefits of Breastfeeding," *Feminist Economics* 3 (1997), 1–24.

36. Centers for Disease Control and Prevention, "Which Infants Are Likely to Be Breastfed?" April 11, 2005, http://www.cdc.gov/pednss/how_to/interpret_data/case_studies/breastfeeding/who.htm.

37. Alice Rossi, "The Biosocial Side of Parenthood," *Human Nature*, June 1978.

38. Becker, *A Treatise*, 32–41.

39. Christina Hoff Sommers, *Who Stole Feminism: How Women Have Betrayed Women* (New York: Simon and Schuster, 1994).

40. Arlie Hochschild with Anne Machung, *The Second Shift: Working Parents and the Revolution at Home* (New York: Viking, 1989); Frances Goldscheider and Linda Waite, *New Families, No Families? The Transformation of the American Home* (Berkeley: University of California Press, 1991); Daphne Spain and Suzanne Bianchi, *Balancing Act: Motherhood, Marriage and Employment among American Women* (New York: Russell Sage Foundation, 1996); A. Walker, "Gender and Family Relationships," in

M. Sussman, S. Steinmetz, and G. Peterson, eds., *Handbook of Marriage and the Family* (New York: Plenum, 1999), 439–474; Liana Sayer, Philip Cohen, and Lynne Casper, *Women, Men and Work* (New York: Russell Sage Foundation, 2004).

41. Julie Brines, "Economic Dependency, Gender, and the Division of Labor at Home," *American Journal of Sociology* 100, no. 3 (1994), 652–688; Amy Kroska, "Division of Domestic Work: Revising and Expanding the Theoretical Explanations," *Journal of Family Issues* 25, no. 7 (October 2004), 900–932; T. N. Greenstein, "Economic Dependence, Gender, and the Division of Labor in the Home: A Replication and Extension," *Journal of Marriage and Family* 62 (2000), 322–335; Michael Bittman, Paula England, Nancy Folbre, and George Matheson, "When Gender Trumps Money: Bargaining and Time in Household Work," working paper no. 221, Institute for Policy Research, Northwestern University, April 4, 2001.

42. Sayer, Cohen, and Casper, *Women, Men and Work.*

43. Other research on family work confirms that wives do a significantly greater share of feminine housework and husbands do a greater share of masculine chores. See, for example, Kroska, "Division of Domestic Work."

44. The variable codes for child care in the 2000 National Survey of Parents are reported in Suzanne Bianchi, Vanessa Wight, and Sara Raley, "Maternal Employment and Family Caregiving: Rethinking Time with Children in the ATUS," paper prepared for the ATUS Early Results Conference, Bethesda, Md., December 9, 2005. The codes for the 1965 Multinational Time Budget Research Project are reported in Suzanne Bianchi, John Robinson, and Melissa Milkie, *Changing Rhythms of American Family Life* (New York: Russell Sage Foundation, 2006), 25.

45. Ann Hulbert, "The Way We Live Now: The Time Trap," *New York Times Magazine,* April 2, 2006.

46. Robert Pear, "Married and Single Parents Spending More Time with Children, Study Finds," *New York Times,* October 17, 2006.

47. For some critical observations on the implications of the "secondary care" construct, see Kimberly Fisher, "Comments on 'Maternal Employment and Family Caregiving: Rethinking Time with Children in the ATUS' by Suzanne Bianchi, Vanessa Wight and Sara Raley," discussant, ATUS Early Results Conference, Bethesda, Md., December 9, 2005.

48. Bianchi, Robinson, and Milkie, *Changing Rhythms,* 62.

49. The proliferation of low-cost modern appliances also has some impact on the time spent on household chores.

50. Sayer, Cohen, and Casper, *Women, Men and Work.*

51. Ibid.

52. Virginia Postrel, "New U.S. Economy: Not Just Buying Stuff," *International Herald Tribune,* September 10, 2004, 17.

53. Stein Ringen, *What Democracy Is For: On Freedom and Moral Government* (Princeton, N.J.: Princeton University Press, 2007), 154.

54. Becker, *A Treatise,* 303.

55. Mark Lino, "Expenditure on Children by Families, 1997," *Family Economics and Nutrition Review* 11, no. 3 (1998), 25–36.

56. Broadwing Capital Advisors, *The Financial Insider* 36, no. 1 (Liberty: Beverly, Mass., 2006). These figures represent the mid-range estimated projections (6 percent inflation) of college costs based on the College Board, *Trends in College Pricing, 2005.*

57. Daniel Cere, "Courtship Today: The View from Academia," *Public Interest* 143 (Spring 2001), 65.

58. Becker, *A Treatise,* 299.

59. Calvin Trillin, "Alice off the Page," *New Yorker,* March 27, 2006, http://www.newyorker.com/archive/2006/03/27/060327fa_fact_trillin.

60. Daniel Kahneman and Amos Tversky, "Prospect Theory: An Analysis of Decision under Risk," *Econometrica* 47, no. 2 (March 1979), 261–291. Extending the ideas of prospect theory, a newer version applies cumulative decision weights, which allow the theory to analyze uncertain choices with any number of outcomes. Amos Tversky and Daniel Kahneman, "Advance in Prospect Theory: Cumulative Representation of Uncertainty," *Journal of Risk and Uncertainty* 5 (1992), 297–323.

61. Kahneman and Tversky also found that in situations where all the choices offer a low probability of winning, people tend to be risk seeking—they select the option that offers the largest gain. Kahneman and Tversky, "Prospect Theory."

62. In most of Europe, thirty is the average age at which women are having their first child. Charlemagne, "The Fertility Bust," *Economist,* February 11, 2006, 50.

63. Amitai Etzioni, *The Moral Dimension: Toward a New Economics* (New York: Free Press, 1988), 95. For a lively discussion of socioeconomics, see Amitai Etzioni, "Toward a New Socio-Economic Paradigm," *Socio-Economic Review* 1, no. 1 (2003), 105–118, followed by comments by Dennis Wrong, Wolfgang Streeck, and J. Rogers Hollingsworth.

Chapter 4. Feminist Expectations

1. L. J. Sax, J. A. Lindholm, A. W. Astin, W. S. Korn, and K. M. Mahoney, *The American Freshman: National Norms for Fall 2001* (Los Angeles: Higher Education Research Institute, UCLA Graduate School of Education and Information Studies, 2001). Also see Tamar Lewin, "At Colleges, Women Are Leaving Men in the Dust," *New York Times,* July 9, 2006.

2. Ilene Lelchuk, "Lots of Toddlers, Few School-Age Kids in S.F.," *San Francisco Chronicle,* May 30, 2006, A1.

3. Lisel Blash et al., "Getting behind the Headlines: Families Leaving San Francisco," Public Research Institute, San Francisco State University, September 2005.

4. Motoko Rich and David Leonhardt, "Saying Goodbye California Sun, Hello Midwest," *New York Times,* November 7, 2005.

5. For further reflections on this index, see Mollie Orshanksy, Harold Watts, Bradley Schiller, and John Korbel, "Measuring Poverty: A Debate," *Public Welfare* 33 (Spring 1978), 46–55.

6. A new data series introduced by the Census Bureau provides a more thorough picture of the resources available to low-income people. When one takes into ac-

count the implicit income from home ownership, estimates of unreported income, and the income of cohabitants, along with welfare payments and food and housing assistance, the poverty rate in 2004 drops from 12.7 percent to 5.1 percent. See Douglas Besharov, "Poor America," *Wall Street Journal,* March 24, 2006, A10.

7. This issue is politically sensitive because federal allocations for social welfare throughout the country often rely on the established measure. If it changes, there are bound to be winners and losers. For a discussion of alternative definitions and technical considerations, see Patricia Ruggles, *Drawing the Line: Alternative Poverty Measures and Their Implications for Public Policy* (Washington, D.C.: Urban Institute Press, 1990); Robert Rector, "The Myth of Widespread Poverty," *Backgrounder,* September 18, 1998; Daniel Weinberg, "Measuring Poverty: Issues and Approaches," Poverty Measurement Working Paper Series, U.S. Census Bureau, December 14, 1995; Constance Citro and Robert Michael, eds., *Measuring Poverty: A New Approach* (Washington, D.C.: National Academy Press, 1995).

8. Robert Rector and Kirk Johnson, "Understanding Poverty in America," *Backgrounder,* January 5, 2004.

9. Pew Research Center, "Luxury or Necessity? Things We Can't Live Without: The List Has Grown in the Past Decade," 2006, http://pewresearch.org.

10. The poverty rates in these countries are usually defined by a relative measure such as the headcount of people earning less than 50 percent of the median income. There are several problems, however, with using median income as a reference point for establishing a poverty line. First, a relatively poor country with a narrow distribution of incomes may have comparatively fewer people earning less than 50 percent of the median income (which would be hard to survive on) than a wealthy country with a much broader range of incomes—thus, by the relative measure Russia has almost the same level of poverty as the United States. Second, a drop in the median income can result in a reduction in the poverty rate, even though the material standard of living of those earning less than 50 percent of the median income has declined—this situation happened in New Zealand between the late 1980s and early 1990s. Finally, in comparisons between European countries and the United States, when incomes are adjusted for purchasing power parity, those at 50 percent of the median income in the United States have a higher level of income than their European counterparts. See, for example, Brian Easton, "Beware the Median," *Social Policy Research Centre Newsletter,* no. 82 (November 2002); Michael Forster and Marco Mira d'Ercole, "Income Distribution and Poverty in OECD Countries in the Second Half of the 1990s," OECD Social, Employment and Migration Working Paper No. 22, Paris, March 10, 2005.

11. William Beveridge, *Social Insurance and Allied Services* (Cmd. 6404) (London: HMSO, 1942).

12. Jens Alber, "The European Social Model and the United States," *European Union Politics* 7, no. 3 (2006), 393–419.

13. Author's calculations based on data from Eurostat, *Eurostat Yearbook: A Statistical Eye on Europe (1987–1997)* (Luxembourg: Office for Official Publications of the European Community, 1999). Germany and Luxembourg were excluded for lack

of data. Average fertility and consumption for 1995 and 1996 do not include Spain and Portugal.

14. Clair Vickery calculated in 1979 that 34 percent of the wife's income in a two-earner family is consumed by work-related expenses and taxes. And Kristin Smith estimates that child-care costs alone take up 20 percent of the income of the poor working mothers who pay for these services. See Clair Vickery, "Women's Economic Contribution to the Family," in Ralph Smith, ed., *The Subtle Revolution: Women at Work* (Washington, D.C.: Urban Institute, 1979); Kristin Smith, "Who's Minding the Kids? Child Care Arrangements: Spring 1997," in U.S. Census Bureau, *Current Population Reports,* July 2002.

15. Standards of quality in child care are by no means absolute. The Child Welfare League of America suggests staff-child ratios of 1:3 for children under the age of three. Child Welfare League of America, *CWLA Standards for Day Care Service* (New York: Child Welfare League of America, 1984). The National Association for the Education of Young Children criteria for accreditation of child-care centers specify adult-child ratios of 1:3 or 1:4 for children under the age of two and 1:4 through 1:6 for children between the ages of two and three. See Suzanne Helbrum and Carollee Howes, "Child Care Cost and Quality," *The Future of Children* 6, no. 2 (Summer–Fall 1996), 62–81.

16. This salary is well below the 2003 average earning of $31,655 for women with some college education but no degree. See U.S. Census Bureau, *Statistical Abstract of the United States: 2006* (Washington, D.C.: Government Printing Office, 2006), 467.

17. In 2003 the median earnings for all women in their longest-held jobs amounted to $22,004, and the median earnings for women working full-time continuously throughout the year amounted to $30,724. Ibid., 429.

18. In about half of the OECD countries, more than 70 percent of the paychecks of low-wage second earners is consumed by taxes, child-care fees, and reduced benefits. For details see Herwig Immervoll and David Barber, "Can Parents Afford to Work? Childcare Costs, Tax-Benefit Policies and Work Incentives," OECD Social, Employment and Migration Working Paper No. 31, Paris, December 15, 2005.

19. For a more detailed description of this brand of feminism, see Neil Gilbert, "Working Families: Hearth to Market," in Mary Ann Mason, Arlene Skolnick, and Stephen Sugarman, eds., *All Our Families: New Policies for a New Century* (New York: Oxford University Press, 2003).

20. Some of the alternative feminist views expressed during this period are discussed in Michael Levin, "Feminism Stage Three," *Commentary* 82, no. 2 (August 1986); Mary Ann Mason, *The Equality Trap* (New York: Simon and Schuster, 1988); Sylvia Ann Hewlett, *A Lesser Life: The Myth of Women's Liberation in America* (New York: William Morrow, 1986); Wendy Kaminer, "Will Class Trump Gender?" *American Prospect* 29 (November–December 1996); Christina Hoff Summers, *Who Stole Feminism: How Women Have Betrayed Women* (New York: Simon and Schuster, 1994), particularly chapter 11 on the Backlash Myth.

21. For a wide-ranging analysis of the current debate about how to legitimize care work and provide caregivers with income security, see Mary Daly, ed., *Care Work: The Quest for Security* (Geneva: International Labour Office, 2001).

22. Anne Alstott, *No Exit: What Parents Owe Their Children and What Society Owes Parents* (New York: Oxford University Press, 2004).

23. Cynthia Fuchs Epstein, "Toward a Family Policy: Changes in Mothers' Loves," in Andrew Cherlin, ed., *The Changing American Family and Public Policy* (Washington, D.C.: Urban Institute, 1988).

24. Louise Tilly and Joan Scott, *Work, Women, and Family,* 2nd ed. (New York: Routledge, 1989), 2.

25. Kaminer, "Will Class Trump Gender?" 48.

26. Mikael Nordenmark, "Does Gender Ideology Explain Differences between Countries Regarding the Involvement of Men and Women in Paid and Unpaid Work?" *International Journal of Social Welfare* 13, no. 3 (July 2004), 233–243.

27. See, for example, Susan Okin, *Justice, Gender, and the Family* (New York: Basic Books, 1992); Constantina Safilios-Rothschild, *Women and Social Policy* (Englewood Cliffs, N.J.: Prentice Hall, 1972).

28. Alan Carlson, "The Curious Case of Gender Equality," *Society* 41, no. 6 (September–October 2004), 30.

29. See Summers, *Who Stole Feminism.* Among the major figures in the gender feminist school of thought included are Gloria Steinem, Patricia Ireland, Susan Faludi, Marilyn French, Naomi Wolf, and Catherine MacKinnon.

30. OECD, *The Integration of Women into the Economy* (Paris: OECD, 1985); OECD, *Shaping Structural Change: The Role of Women* (Paris: OECD, 1991).

31. Lane Kenworthy, *Egalitarian Capitalism: Jobs, Income and Growth in Affluent Countries* (New York: Russell Sage Foundation, 2004).

32. Barbara Bergmann, "Subsidizing Child Care by Mothers at Home," *Feminist Economics* 6 (2000), 78.

33. For a highly constructive analysis of the needs of, and relevant policy responses for, women on the fast track, see Mary Ann Mason and Eve Mason Ekman, *Mothers on the Fast Track: How a New Generation Can Balance Family and Careers* (New York: Oxford University Press, 2007).

34. Michael Cahlin, "Recareerists," MSN Encarta Premium, http://encarta.msn.com/encnet/departments/adultlearning/?article=recareerists. It should be noted that the survey cited here was conducted for Phoenix University, which delivers online adult education. The fact that the survey findings support that institution's general mission does not invalidate the results, but it deserves mention.

35. U.S. Department of Education, National Center for Education Statistics, *Digest of Educational Statistics 2005* (Washington, D.C.: U.S. Dept. of Education, 2005), table 172.

36. My view of "temporal autonomy" as the freedom to choose when to work and what work to perform is a bit more restrictive than the use of this term to denote "freedom to spend one's time as one will, outside the daily necessities of life." See, for example, Robert Goodin, Antti Parpo, and Olli Kangas, "The Temporal Welfare State: The Case of Finland," *Journal of Social Policy* 33, no. 4 (2004), 531–552.

37. Paul Graham, "What Business Can Learn from Open Source," August 2005, http://www.paulgraham.com/opensource.html.

38. Daniel Bell, *The End of Ideology* (New York: Free Press, 1960), 231.

39. In the OECD countries, the average number of hours worked per year was only 1,700 hours. Paul Swaim and Pascal Marianna, "Clocking In and Clocking Out: Recent Trends in Working Hours," *OECD Observer,* October 2004.

40. For an insider's satirical view of how academics dodge committee assignments while elevating their reputation for analytic rigor, see Harris Bullford, "Scaling the Ivory Tower: How to Avoid Committee Service," *Change: The Magazine of Higher Learning* (January–February 1988), 48–49.

41. Some might take this as a criticism of the professoriate by a disgruntled member of the community. Thus, for the record, I should say that my assessment here is offered not as a criticism but as a description—by someone who has been treated far better in academic life than he probably deserves.

42. The international networking in the conference circuits of academic life is amusingly portrayed in David Lodge, *Small World* (New York: Penguin Books, 1995).

43. Tom Lutz, "The Summer Next Time," *New York Times,* September 4, 2006.

44. Wendy Kaminer, *A Fearful Freedom: Women's Flight from Equality* (New York: Addison-Wesley, 1990).

45. Betty Friedan, *The Feminine Mystique* (New York: Dell Publishing, 1963). Friedan's phrase was perhaps a riff on the well-known lament about the oppression of homosexuality. The "love that dare not speak its name" comes from the poem "Two Loves" by Lord Alfred Douglas, who was Oscar Wilde's lover. The line is sometimes attributed to Wilde (whose aphorisms are legendary) because of the interpretation he offered in court during his trial for homosexual sodomy—of which he was convicted and imprisoned.

46. Dan Seligman, "The Friedan Mystique," *Commentary* 121, no. 4 (April 2006), 42–46.

47. Elizabeth Fox-Genovese, "The Feminist Mistake," American Enterprise Institute Bradley Lecture Series, Washington, D.C., October 4, 1993.

48. George Bernard Shaw, *The Intelligent Woman's Guide to Socialism and Capitalism* (New Brunswick, N.J.: Aldine Transaction, 1984; originally published in 1928), 176.

49. Suzanne Gordon, "Feminism and Caring," *American Prospect,* Summer 1992, 127.

50. Fox-Genovese observes that "the primary mission of contemporary feminism has been to free women from oppressive domestic roles." "The Feminist Mistake," 12.

51. Liana Sayer, Philip Cohen, and Lynne Casper, *Women, Men, and Work* (New York: Russell Sage Foundation, 2004), 1.

52. Linda Hirshman, "Homeward Bound," *American Prospect,* December 2005.

53. Meghan Cox Gurdon, "She's Back! Meghan Cox Gurdon on the New Housewife," *Women's Quarterly* 15 (1998), 5.

54. Daniel Kahneman et al., "A Survey Method for Characterizing Daily Life Experience: The Day Reconstruction Method," *Science* 306 (December 2004), 1176–1780.

55. Pew Research Center, "As Marriage and Parenthood Drift Apart, Public

Is Concerned about Social Impact," July 1, 2007, http://pewresearch.org/pubs/526/marriage-parenthood.

56. Christina Maslach, "Burned-Out," *Human Behavior* 5 (1976), 99–113; H. J. Freudenberger, "Staff Burnout," *Journal of Social Issues* 30 (1974), 159–165.

57. Tom Cox, Mary Tisserand, and Toon Taris, "The Conceptualization and Measurement of Burnout: Questions and Directions," *Work and Stress* 19, no. 3 (September 2005), 187–191.

58. OECD, *Ageing and Income: Financial Resources and Retirement in 9 OECD Countries* (OECD: Paris, 2001). The countries include Canada, Finland, Germany, Italy, the Netherlands, Sweden, Japan, the United Kingdom, and the United States. Japan, with relatively high rates of employment among elderly men, is an outlier among this group. In 1999, 91 percent of Japanese men ages fifty-five to fifty-nine were employed, compared to the nine-country average of 69.2 percent, and 66 percent of Japanese men ages sixty to sixty-four were employed, compared to the nine-country average of 40.6 percent.

59. Ibid.

60. Johannes Siegrist, "Work, Health and Welfare: New Challenges," *International Journal of Social Welfare* 15, supp. 1 (July 2006), S5–S12. Also see M. Elovainio et al., "Job Demands and Job Control as Correlates of Early Retirement Thoughts in Finnish Social and Healthcare Employees," *Work and Stress* 19 (2005), 84–92.

61. *Newsweek* Poll conducted by Princeton Survey Research Associates, June 24–25, 1999, http://www.pollingreport.com/work.htm.

62. William M. Runyan, "Psychobiography and the Psychology of Science: Understanding Relations between the Life and Work of Individual Psychologists," *Review of General Psychology* 10, no. 2 (2006), 147–162. Runyan notes, however, that those who have studied Freud's life disagree about the extent to which his conception of the Oedipus complex was shaped by self-analysis, political expediency, clinical patients, and other factors.

63. Karl Marx, *Das Kapital,* edited by Friedrich Engels and condensed by Serge Levitsky (Chicago: Henry Regnery, 1959), 248.

64. Sigmund Freud, *Civilization and Its Discontents* (New York: W. W. Norton, 1961), 27.

65. Robert Sutton, *The No Asshole Rule: How to Build a Civilized Workplace and Surviving One That Isn't* (New York: Warner Business Books, 2007).

66. Neil Gilbert, *Welfare Justice: Restoring Social Equity* (New Haven: Yale University Press, 1995).

67. Alan Wolfe, *Whose Keeper? Social Science and Moral Obligation* (Berkeley: University of California Press, 1989), 141–142.

68. "Sex Society and the Female Dilemma: A Dialogue between Betty Friedan and Simone de Beauvoir," *Saturday Review,* June 14, 1975, 18. Cited in Summers, *Who Stole Feminism,* 256–257.

69. Hirshman, "Homeward Bound." Hirshman's advice for women to marry down as a way of finding husbands who will do an equal share of the housework is provocative, but it lacks empirical verification. As I noted in Chapter 3, a good deal of

research confirms that men who earn less than their wives tend to perform a smaller share of the housework than those earning more than their wives.

Chapter 5. How Family Friendly Are Family-Friendly Policies?

1. Testimony of Douglas Besharov before the Subcommittee on Twenty-first-Century Competitiveness of the Committee on Education and Workforce, February 27, 2002. The original version of this testimony appeared in Douglas Besharov and Nazanin Samuri, "Child Care after Welfare Reform," in Rebecca Blank and Ron Haskins, eds., *The New World of Welfare* (Washington, D.C.: Brookings Institution Press, 2001), 461–481.

2. The $16 billion in publicly subsidized care amounts to less than half of what is spent privately for day care. When private spending on child care is added in, total U.S. spending climbs to about $50 billion, which covers the expenses of about 12 million children. Douglas Besharov and Jeffrey Morrow, "Rethinking Child Care," *Evaluation Review* 30, no. 5 (October 2006), 539–555.

3. Commission on Children at Risk, "Report to the Nation," *Hardwired to Connect: The New Scientific Case for Authoritative Communities* (New York: Institute for American Values, 2003), 48.

4. An eight-year withdrawal assumes that the two children were spaced two years apart and started going to school for a full day at age six.

5. Since the late 1980s the percentage of public schools offering extended-day programs—before and after school—has more than tripled. In addition to provisions funded by the states, federal aid for after-school programs authorized in 1994 is currently at $1 billion. Beyond providing a supervised place for children to stay after school, the benefits of these programs are uncertain, and there is some evidence of negative impacts on behavior. An impressive national experiment evaluating federally supported after-school programs in twelve school districts found that although the children in these programs felt safer than those in the control groups, they experienced no academic gains and displayed higher levels of negative behavior resulting in suspensions from school, teachers reporting the behavior to parents, and students being disciplined by teachers. The differences between the experimental and control groups on the negative outcomes were measurable but not large—ranging from effect sizes of 0.12 to 0.16. See Susanne James-Burdumy et al., U.S. Department of Education, National Center for Education Evaluation and Regional Assistance, *When Schools Stay Open Late: The National Evaluation of the 21st Century Community Learning Centers Program: Final Report* (Washington, D.C.: Government Printing Office, 2005).

6. An analysis of twenty-one large-scale, public, early-childhood education programs showed that most of them provided a part-day service for children beginning at age four. W. Steven Barnett, "Long-Term Effects of Early Childhood Programs on Cognitive and School Outcomes," *The Future of Children* 5, no. 3 (Winter 1995), 25–50.

7. The Perry Preschool program is legendary for several reasons, not the least of which is that its oft-cited findings revealed a remarkable impact of early education on poor children. The model project randomly assigned students to the preschool and control groups, offered an exceptionally high-quality preschool experience, and was linked to a longitudinal study that followed the participants for twenty-five years. See Barnett, "Long-Term Effects of Early Childhood Programs"; W. Steven Barnett, "Benefit-Cost Analysis of Preschool Education: Findings from a 25-Year Follow-Up," *American Journal of Orthopsychiatry* 63, no. 4 (October 1993), 500–508; David Blau and Janet Curie, "Preschool Day Care and Afterschool Care: Who's Minding the Kids," National Bureau of Economic Research Working Paper 10670, August 2004.

8. James Q. Wilson, "In Loco Parentis," *Brookings Review,* Fall 1993, 12–15.

9. Jay Belsky and L. D. Steinberg, "The Effects of Day Care: A Critical Review," *Child Development* 49 (1978), 929–949.

10. These conclusions are expressed in three independent reviews of the early research literature on child care: Kristin Moore and Sandra Hofferth, "Women and Their Children," in Ralph Smith, ed., *The Subtle Revolution* (Washington, D.C.: Urban Institute, 1979), 125–158; Barbara Heyns, "The Influence of Parents' Work on Children's School Achievement," in Edward Zigler and Edmund Gordon, eds., *Day Care: Scientific and Social Policy Issues* (Boston: Auburn House, 1982); Jacqueline Lerner and Nancy Galambos, "Child Development and Family Change: The Influences of Maternal Employment on Infants and Toddlers," in Lewis Lipisitt and Carolyn Rovee-Collier, eds., *Advances in Infancy Research,* vol. 4 (Hillsdale, N.J.: Ablex, 1986).

11. This conclusion was drawn from Elizabeth Harvey, "Short-Term and Long-Term Effects of Early Parental Employment on Children of the National Longitudinal Survey of Youth," *Developmental Psychology,* March 1999, 445–459.

12. For a critical assessment of the study see Brian Robertson, *Day Care Deception: What the Child Care Establishment Isn't Telling Us* (San Francisco: Encounter Books, 2003).

13. Quoted in Carol Krucoff, "The Effects of Day Care on Children," *Washington Post,* December 27, 1985.

14. Deborah Fallows, *A Mother's Work* (Boston: Houghton Mifflin, 1985). Also see Angela Browne Miller, *The Day Care Dilemma: Critical Concerns for American Families* (New York: Insight Books, 1990).

15. See, for example, "Nonmaternal Care and Family Factors in Early Development: An Overview of the NICHD Study of Early Child Care," *Applied Developmental Psychology* 22 (2001), 457–492; "Early Child Care and Children's Development Prior to School Entry: Results from the NICHD Study of Early Child Care," *American Educational Research Journal* 39, no. 1 (Spring 2002), 133–164; "Does Quality of Child Care Affect Child Outcomes at Age 4 1/2?" *Developmental Psychology* 39, no. 3 (2003), 451–469; "Child Care Structure, Process, Outcome: Direct and Indirect Effects of Child-Care Quality on Young Children's Development," *Psychological Sciences* 13, no.3 (May 2002), 199–206; "Does the Amount of Time Spent in Child Care Predict Socioemotional Adjustment during the Transition to Kindergarten?" *Child Development* 74, no. 4 (July–August 2003), 976–994; all by the NICHD Early Child Care Research Net-

work. Also see Jeanne Brooks-Gunn, Wen-Jui Han, and Jane Waldfogel, "Maternal Employment and Child Cognitive Outcomes in the First Three Years of Life: The NICHD Study of Early Child Care," *Child Development* 73, no. 4 (July–August 2002), 1052–1072; Deborah Lowe Vandell, "Early Child Care: The Known and the Unknown," *Merrill-Palmer Quarterly* 50, no. 3 (July 2004), 387–414.

16. Judith Langlois and Lynn Liben, "Child Care Research: An Editorial Perspective," *Child Development* 27, no. 4 (July–August 2003), 969–975.

17. For a rigorous analytic review of the issues, see Douglas Besharov and Jeffrey Morrow, "Rethinking Child Care Research," *Evaluation Review* 30, no. 5 (October 2006), 539–555; and the other articles in this issue, particularly Greg Duncan and Christina Gibson-Davis, "Connecting Child Care Quality to Child Outcomes," 611–630.

18. Selma Fraiberg, *Every Child's Birthright: In Defense of Mothering* (New York: Basic Books, 1977), 111.

19. Belsky and Steinberg, "The Effects of Day Care"; Jay Belsky, L. D. Steinberg, and A. Walker, "The Ecology of Day Care," in M. Lamb, ed., *Childrearing in Nontraditional Families* (Hillsdale, N.J.: Erlbaum, 1982).

20. Jay Belsky, "Infant Day Care: A Cause for Concern?" *Zero to Three: Bulletin of the National Center for Clinical Infant Studies* 6, no. 5 (September 1986), 6. Also see Jay Belsky, "The Effects of Infant Care Reconsidered," *Early Childhood Research Quarterly* 3 (1988), 235–272.

21. NICHD Early Child Care Research Network, "The Effects of Infant Child Care on Infant-Mother Attachment: Results from the NICHD Study of Early Child Care," *Child Development* 68 (1997), 860–879.

22. NICHD Early Child Care Research Network, "Child Care and Family Predictors of Preschool Attachment and Stability from Infancy," *Developmental Psychology* 37 (2001), 847–862.

23. NICHD Early Child Care Research Network, "Nonmaternal Care and Family Factors in Early Development," 483.

24. The findings from these studies—the Cost Quality and Outcome Study, and the National Child Care Staffing Study—are reported in Blau and Curie, "Preschool Day Care."

25. NICHD Early Child Care Research Network, "Child-Care and Mother-Child Interaction in the First Three Years of Life," *Developmental Psychology* 35 (1999), 1399–1413.

26. Vandell, "Early Child Care."

27. NICHD Early Child Care Research Network, "Overview of Early Child Care Effects at 4.5 Years," paper presented at the Early Child Care and Children's Development Prior to School Entry symposium, conducted at the Biennial Meeting of the Society for Research in Child Development, Minneapolis, Minn., April 2001; NICHD Early Child Care Research Network, "Further Exploration of the Detected Effects of Quantity of Early Child Care on Socio-Emotional Adjustment," paper presented at the Early Child Care and Children's Development Prior to School Entry symposium, conducted at the Biennial Meeting of the Society for Research in Child Development, Minneapolis, Minn., April 2001.

28. For a balanced discussion of how these findings were interpreted in the media, see Statistical Assessment Service, "The Good News and the Bad News on Day-care: Perspective Matters," *Vital STATS: Newsletter of the Statistical Assessment Service,* June 2001, 1.

29. Vandell, "Early Child Care." The average problem-behavior scores for children rose with the hours per week in care (zero to nine, ten to twenty-nine, thirty to forty-five, and more than forty-five hours).

30. NICHD Early Child Care Research Network, "Does the Amount of Time Spent in Child Care Predict Socioemotional Adjustment."

31. NICHD Early Child Care Research Network, "Early Child Care and Children's Development in the Primary Grades: Follow-Up Results from the NICHD Study of Early Child Care," *American Educational Research Journal* 45 (2005), 537–570.

32. However, when the dose-response relationship between quality of care and measures of cognitive ability was examined, the findings showed no effects in the expected direction. That is, more exposure to high-quality care did not yield higher performance on the outcome measures. NICHD Early Child Care Research Network, "Does Quality of Child Care Affect Child Outcomes at Age 4 1/2?"

33. See, for example, Susanna Loeb et al., "How Much Is Too Much? The Influence of Preschool Centers on Children's Development Nationwide: Summary," paper presented at the Association for Policy Analysis and Management Meeting, Washington, D.C., November 4, 2005 (forthcoming in *Economics of Education Review*); Katherine Magnuson et al., "Inequality in Children's School Readiness and Public Funding," *Focus* 42, no. 1 (Fall 2005), 12–18.

34. Loeb et al. report overall gains in academic skills that amounted to an "effect size" of .10 Standard Deviation (SD) and about .20 SD for the poorest children. Loeb et al., "How Much Is Too Much." For a sense of this magnitude, consider that an effect size of .20 SD would yield a three-point increase on a standard IQ scale (which has a mean of 100 and an SD of 15). According to the widely cited standards formulated by J. Cohen, an effect size of .20 SD is small. See Cohen, *Statistical Power Analysis for the Behavioral Sciences,* 2nd ed. (Hillsdale, N.J.: Erlbaum, 1988). The NICHD found that the effect size of child-care quality on cognitive outcomes "if any, is not large (approximately .20)." NICHD Early Child Care Research Network, "Does Quality of Child Care Affect Child Outcomes at Age 4 1/2?"

35. Magnuson et al. found that 60–80 percent of the cognitive gains linked to preschool attendance had dissipated by the spring of the first grade. Magnuson et al., "Inequality in Children's School Readiness." Barnett reports variable effects, with weak evidence for persistent achievement and some indication that the most disadvantaged children experienced the largest benefits. Barnett, "Long-Term Effects of Early Childhood Programs."

36. Compared to those in the control group who did not attend preschool, the Perry Preschool students also scored higher on educational achievement tests at ages nine and fourteen and were less likely to be classified as mentally retarded—these differences were statistically significant. The Perry Preschool students were on average three and a half years old, had an average Child's Stanford-Binet IQ score of 79.6, and

came from disadvantaged families, in which the majority of parents were on welfare and had not graduated from high school. The program was staffed with a ratio of six children to one certified teacher, typically with training in child development. Research on other model programs of early intervention showed generally positive results though not always on academic achievement tests. For a review of the research on these developmentally oriented programs see Barnett, "Long-Term Effects of Early Childhood Programs"; Barnett, "Benefit-Cost Analysis of Preschool Education"; Blau and Curie, "Preschool Day Care."

37. U.S. Department of Labor, Bureau of Labor Statistics, "Occupational Outlook Handbook," http://www.bls.gov/oco/ocos170.htm.

38. See, for example, the review of the evidence by Anne Hungerford and Martha Cox, "Family Factors in Child Care Research," *Evaluation Review* 30, no. 5 (October 2006), 631–655; W. Norton Grubb, "Families and Schools Raising Children: The Inequitable Effects of Family Background on Schooling Outcomes," in Jill Duerr Berrick and Neil Gilbert, eds., *Raising Children: Emerging Needs, Modern Risks, and Social Responses* (New York: Oxford University Press, forthcoming).

39. See, for example, the impact on social development analyzed in Loeb et al., "How Much Is Too Much"; Sandra Scarr and Marlene Eisenberg, "Child Care Research: Issues, Perspectives and Results," *Annual Review of Psychology* 44 (1993), 613–644.

40. Janet Gornick, Marcia Meyers, and Katherine Ross, "Supporting the Employment of Mothers: Policy Variations across Fourteen Welfare States," *Journal of European Social Policy* 7, no. 1 (February 1997), 45–70.

41. George Weigel, "Europe's Two Culture Wars," *Commentary* 121, no. 5 (May 2006), 29–36.

42. United Nations, *World Population Prospects: The 2004 Revision Highlights* (New York: United Nations, 2005).

43. Richard Easterlin, *Birth and Fortune: The Impact of Numbers on Personal Welfare* (Chicago: University of Chicago Press, 1980).

44. See, for example, Fred Pampel and H. Elizabeth Peters, "The Easterlin Effect," *Annual Review of Sociology* 21 (1995), 163–194; John Cleland and Christopher Wilson, "Demand Theories of the Fertility Transition: An Iconoclastic View," *Population Studies* 41, no. 1 (March 1987).

45. Gosta Esping-Andersen, *Social Foundations of Post-industrial Economies* (Oxford: Oxford University Press, 1999), 68.

46. These positive findings ($r = .480$) are based on my analysis of data from Eurostat, *Eurostat Yearbook: A Statistical Eye on Europe* (Luxembourg: Office for Official Publications of the European Communities, 1999).

47. For a discussion of these trends, see Gerda Neyer, "Family Policies and Low Fertility in Western Europe," Max Planck Institute for Demographic Research Working Paper 2003–021, Rostock, Germany, July 2003.

48. Molly Moore, "More Longtime Couples in France Prefer L'Amour without Marriage," *Washington Post*, November 21, 2006, A22.

49. The seventeen major OECD countries in this analysis were selected to represent the well-known classification of welfare-state regimes developed in Gosta

Esping-Andersen, *The Three Worlds of Welfare Capitalism* (Princeton, N.J.: Princeton University Press, 1990); and elaborated in his *Social Foundations of Post-industrial Economies.* The countries are classified as follows: *social-democratic*—Denmark, Finland, Norway, Sweden; *conservative*—Austria, Belgium, France, Germany, the Netherlands; *liberal*—Australia, Canada, Ireland, the United Kingdom, the United States; *southern European*—Italy, Portugal, Spain.

50. For a more detailed analysis of this pattern of convergence on family-friendly expenditures among welfare-state regimes, see Jing Guo and Neil Gilbert, "Welfare State Regimes and Family Policy: A Longitudinal Analysis," *International Journal of Social Welfare* 16 (2007).

51. In this regard, Walter Korpi distinguishes the *general support model* of family-oriented benefits, which is characterized, for example, by children's allowances and family tax benefits, from the *dual-earner support model,* which emphasizes day-care services for young children and maternity/paternity leave provisions. Walter Korpi, "Faces of Inequality: Gender, Class, and Patterns of Inequalities in Different Types of Welfare States," Luxembourg Income Study Working Paper No. 224, Center for the Study of Population, Poverty and Public Policy, Differdange, Luxembourg, February 2000.

52. These differences are analyzed in Rianne Mahon, "Child Care: Toward What Kind of 'Social Europe'?" *Social Politics,* Fall 2002, 343–379.

53. Numerous studies have described the variations in family policies and compared measures in different countries. See, for example, W. Dumon, ed., *National Family Policies in EU Countries in 1991* (Brussels: Commission of the European Communities, 1992); J. S. Hyde and M. Essex, eds., *Parental Leave and Child Care: Setting a Research and Policy Agenda* (Philadelphia: Temple University Press, 1991); Sheila Kamerman and Alfred Kahn, eds., *Family Policy: Government and Families in Fourteen Countries* (New York: Columbia University Press, 1978); Sheila Kamerman and Alfred Kahn, *Child Care, Parental Leave, and the Under 3s: Policy Innovation in Europe* (New York: Auburn House, 1991); Ingalil Montanari, "From Family Wage to Marriage Subsidy and Child Benefits: Controversy and Consensus in the Development of Child Support," *Journal of European Social Policy* 10, no. 4 (November 2000), 307–333; Wim van Oorschot, "Work, Welfare, and Citizenship: Activation and Flexicurity in the Netherlands," Dept. of Sociology, Tilburg University, 2002; Howard Palley and Elizabeth Bowman, "A Comparison of National Family Policies: France and Sweden," *Children and Youth Services Review* 24, no. 5 (May 2002), 345–373; R. Rosenfeld and G. Birkelund, "Women's Part-Time Work: A Cross-National Comparison," *European Sociological Review* 11, no. 2 (1995), 111–134.

54. For a discussion of this development in the United States, see Stanley Surrey, *Pathways to Tax Reform* (Cambridge, Mass.: Harvard University Press, 1974).

55. For one of the earliest efforts to reformulate an empirical index of social expenditure that would account for the true cost and value of all social-welfare benefits, see Neil Gilbert and Ailee Moon, "Analyzing Welfare Effort: An Appraisal of Comparative Methods," *Journal of Policy Analysis and Management* 7 (1988), 326–340. This index demonstrated a significant shift in social expenditure rankings among coun-

tries, which occurred when the analysis controlled for tax burden, tax expenditures, and need.

56. Willem Adema et al., "Net Public Social Expenditure," Labour Market and Social Policy Occasional Paper No. 19, OECD, Paris, 1996. Their net total expenditure index represents the cumulative value of benefits distributed through direct public expenditures, tax expenditures, and publicly mandated private expenditures, reduced by direct and indirect taxes on these benefits, and adds in the value of voluntary private expenditures, reduced by direct and indirect taxes.

57. Irwin Garfinkel, Lee Rainwater, and Timothy Smeeding, "Equal Opportunities for Children: Social Welfare Expenditures in English-Speaking Countries and Western Europe," *Focus* 23, no. 3 (Spring 2005), 16–23.

58. Gerda Neyer, "Family Policies and Low Fertility," 32.

59. Janet Gornick, "Overworked, Time Poor, and Abandoned by Uncle Sam: Why Don't Americans Protest?" *Dissent Magazine*, Summer 2005. For the empirical comparisons, see Janet Gornick and Marcia Meyers, *Families That Work: Policies for Reconciling Parenthood and Employment* (New York: Russell Sage Foundation, 2003).

60. In 1997, 31 percent of dual-earner couples with children under fourteen had at least one parent with a work schedule that differed from the standard five-day-a-week, 9-to-5 schedule. Ronald Rindfuss, Karen Guzzo, and S. Philip Morgan, "The Changing Institutional Context of Low Fertility," *Population Research and Policy Review* 22 (2003), 416.

61. Gornick and Meyers, *Families That Work*, 273–274.

62. Joan Williams, *Unbending Gender: Why Family and Work Conflict and What to Do About It* (New York: Oxford University Press, 2000).

63. Daphne Spain and Suzanne Bianchi, *Balancing Act: Motherhood, Marriage, and Employment among American Women* (New York: Russell Sage Foundation, 1996).

64. Rindfuss, Guzzo, and Morgan, "The Changing Institutional Context." Also see S. Philip Morgan, "Is Low Fertility a 21st Century Crisis?" *Demography* 40, no. 4 (2003), 589–603.

65. Morgan, "Is Low Fertility a 21st Century Crisis?" 596.

66. F. C. Billari and H. P. Kohler, "Patterns of Low and Lowest-Low Fertility in Europe," *Population Studies* 58, no. 2 (2004), 161–176. Low fertility rates in Spain have been explained by the high unemployment rates for young adults and their tendency to remain living at home with their parents longer than in other European countries. See Jonathan Grant et al., *Low Fertility and Aging: Causes, Consequences, and Policy Options* (Santa Monica: RAND, 2004).

67. Marie-Therese Letablier, "The Work-Family Relationship: A European Perspective," paper presented at the European Regional Meeting of the International Social Security Association, Luxembourg, May 19–21, 1999.

68. Alvin Schorr, "Income Maintenance and the Birth Rate," *Social Security Bulletin* 28, no. 12 (December 1965), 2–10.

69. Joelle Sleebos, "Low Fertility Rates in OECD Countries: Facts and Policy Responses," OECD Social, Employment, and Migration Working Paper No. 15, Paris, 2003.

70. This viewpoint is confirmed in Ronald Inglehart and Wayne Baker, "Modernization, Cultural Change, and the Persistence of Cultural Values," *American Sociological Review* 65 (February 2000), 19–51. Also see Seymour Lipset, *American Exceptionalism* (New York: Norton, 1996).

71. Comparing U.S. to Italian fertility rates, Morgan offers a hypothetical model that illustrates how small differences in factors such as intended family size, unwanted pregnancies, timing of first births, infecundity, and decisions to revise childbearing intentions because of life experiences might account for substantial differences in fertility. Morgan, "Is Low Fertility a 21st Century Crisis?"

72. Jane Lewis, "Men, Women, Work, and Care Policies," *Journal of European Social Policy* 16, no. 4 (November 2006), 390.

73. Swedish Institute, *Child Care in Sweden* (Stockholm: Swedish Institute, 1992).

74. Patricia Morgan, *Family Policy, Family Changes: Sweden, Italy and Britain Compared* (London: Civitas, 2006), 55.

75. Alan Wolfe, *Whose Keeper? Social Science and Moral Obligation* (Berkeley: University of California Press, 1989), 142.

76. David Popenoe, "Marriage and the Family: What Does the Scandinavian Experience Tell Us?" *The State of Our Unions 2005* (Piscataway, N.J.: National Marriage Project, 2005).

Chapter 6. Rethinking Family Policy

1. See, for example, Janet Gornick and Marcia Meyers, *Families That Work: Policies for Reconciling Parenthood and Employment* (New York: Russell Sage, 2003); Ronald Rindfuss and Karin Brewster, "Childrearing and Fertility," *Population and Development Review* 22 (1996), 258–289. They suggest that "anything that decreases the accessibility, quality, or acceptability of existing childcare arrangements or substantially increased the cost of childcare would likely lead to a swift decline in fertility" (283).

2. On the matter of child care, it is difficult to find family policy analysts in the United States who advise anything other than trying to replicate the European experience. For a typical statement, see Marcia Meyers and Janet Gornick, "The European Model," *American Prospect* 11, no. 15 (November 2004), A21–A22.

3. David Kirp, "You're Doing Fine, Oklahoma!" *American Prospect* 15, no. 1 (November 2004).

4. For an analysis of the Dutch system, see Wim Van Oorschot, "Dutch 'Flexicurity' Policy: Flexibility and Security for Dutch Workers?" paper presented at the Fourth International Research Conference on Social Security, Antwerp, May 5–7, 2003.

5. Jane Lewis draws attention to the important distinction between macro institutional adjustments, which involve statutory policies of the state, and micro adjustments, which include voluntary measures at the level of the firm. She notes some evidence that suggests that the promotion of voluntary measures is unlikely to reconcile work and family life in the absence of statutory commitments. See Jane Lewis,

"Men, Women, Work, Care, and Policies," *European Journal of Social Policy* 16, no. 4 (November 2006), 387–392. Also see Matthew Gray and Jacqueline Tudball, *Family-Friendly Work Practices: Differences within and between Workplaces* (Melbourne: Australian Institute of Family Studies, 2002).

6. For an insightful discussion of faculty experiences, see Mary Ann Mason and Eve Mason Ekman, *Mothers on the Fast Track: How a New Generation Can Balance Family and Careers* (New York: Oxford University Press, 2007).

7. OECD, *The Integration of Women into the Economy* (Paris: OECD, 1985), 141.

8. John Ekberg, Rickard Eriksson, and Guido Friebel, "Parental Leave: A Policy Evaluation of the Swedish 'Daddy-Month' Reform," IZA Discussion Paper No. 1617, June 2005 (available at the Social Science Research Network Web site, http://ssrn.com/abstract=728444); OECD, *Babies and Bosses: Reconciling Work and Family Life*, vol. 3 (Paris: OECD, 2004).

9. Elina Schleutker, "Is It Commodification, De-commodification, Familialism or De-familialization? Parental Leave in Sweden and Finland," working paper no. 31, Institut fur Politikwissenschaft, Universitat Tübingen, Ger., 2006.

10. Ekberg, Eriksson, and Friebel, "Parental Leave," 4.

11. Ibid. This study conformed neatly to the standards of a natural experiment, lending much credibility to the findings.

12. Schleutker, "Is It Commodification." The 2005 proposal was still under consideration in 2006.

13. Rudy Ray Seward, Dale E. Yeatts, Lisa K. Zottarelli, "Parental Leave and Father Involvement in Child Care: Sweden and the United States," *Journal of Comparative Family Studies* 33, no. 3 (2002), 387–395.

14. Fabrizio Bernardi, "Public Policies and Low Fertility: Rationales for Public Intervention and a Diagnosis for the Spanish Case," *Journal of European Social Policy* 15, no. 2 (May 2005), 123–138.

15. U.S. Department of Labor, Bureau of Labor Statistics, *Current Population Surveys: 1988–2005 Annual Social and Economic Supplements.*

16. See, for example, the proposals for a caretaker resource account and life-planning insurance in Anne Alstott, *No Exit: What Parents Owe Their Children and What Society Owes Parents* (New York: Oxford University Press, 2004). Finnish pluralism, where three-quarters of children under age three and one-third of those over age three are cared for at home, is described by Anneli Anttonen, "The Politics of Social Care in Finland: Child and Elder Care in Transition," in Mary Daly, ed., *Care Work: The Quest for Security* (Geneva: International Labour Office, 2001), 143–158. Also see Daniel McGinn, "Getting Back on Track," *Newsweek*, September 25, 2006, 62–63.

17. Constitution of Ireland, Articles 41.2.1 and 41.2.2.

18. "The Still-Small Voice of Ireland," submitted to the All-Party Oireachtas Committee on the Constitution. For more discursive expressions of the debate, see Nora Bennis, "Art. 41.2.1 and 41.2.2: Mothers' Rights Article—An Unchanging, Timeless, Self-Evident, Universal Principle—Time to Choose," address to the All-Party Oireachtas Committee on Constitution, Leinster House, April 26, 2005; Liam O Gogain, "A Vision for Sustainable Society, the Family, Parenting and the Irish Consti-

tution," submission to the All-Party Oireachtas Committee on Constitution on behalf of Parental Equality, April 27, 2005, www.parentalequality.ie.

19. OECD, *OECD Factbook 2006: Economic, Environmental and Social Statistics* (Paris: OECD, 2006), 103.

20. An even more radical, if less likely, possibility is that modern technology—computers, robotics, telecommunications—will alter the very need for mass employment and work as we know it. This scenario of a workerless economy is developed by Jeremy Rifkin, *The End of Work: The Decline of the Global Labor Force and the Dawn of the Post-Market Era* (New York: G. P. Putnam's Sons, 1995).

21. McGinn, "Getting Back on Track."

22. Pew Research Center, "Fewer Mothers Prefer Full-Time Work: From 1997 to 2007," http://pewresearch.org.pubs/536/working-women.

23. For analysis of these programs in Austria, Germany, Luxembourg, Sweden, and the United Kingdom, as well the experimental U.S. programs providing cash benefits for elderly care in Arkansas, Florida, and New Jersey, see Jens Lundsgaard, "Consumer Directions and Choice in Long-Term Care for Older Persons, Including Payments for Informal Care: Is It Good for Care Outcomes, Employment and Fiscal Sustainability?" paper presented at the Consumerism of Care for the Elderly symposium, Danish National Institute for Social Research, Copenhagen, August 30, 2004.

24. For an earlier version of the proposal for a home-care allowance, see Neil Gilbert, "In Support of Domesticity: A Neglected Family Policy Option," *Journal of Policy Analysis and Management* 2, no. 4 (Summer 1983), 628–631.

25. Molly Ladd-Taylor, *Mother-at-Work: Women, Child Welfare, and the State, 1890 to 1930* (Urbana: University of Illinois Press, 1994), 145.

26. At the top of the list were proposals calling for work-related reforms such as family-leave policy. See White House Conference on Families, *Listening to America's Families: Action of the 80s, Summary of the Report to the President, Congress, and Families in the Nation* (Washington, D.C.: Government Printing Office, 1980).

27. William J. Byron, "Paid Homemaking: An Idea in Search of a Policy," *USA Today,* July 1984, 84.

28. For example, see Allan Carlson and David Blankenhorn, "Marriage and Taxes: The Case for Family-Friendly Taxation," *Weekly Standard,* February 9, 1998.

29. For examples of the typical policy discourse focused on enabling the employment of mothers with young children, see Karen Christopher, "Family-Friendly Europe," *American Prospect,* April 8, 2002, 59–61; Janet Gornick, "Reconcilable Differences," *American Prospect,* April 8, 2002, 42–46.

30. In Germany, Christian Leipert and Michael Opielka argue for a new social contract based on the understanding that parental child-care work is functionally equivalent to gainful employment. Calculating the monetary value of child care, they propose a monthly salary of approximately $1,360 for the first child and $680 for additional children up to age seven. Although this proposal stirred some debate in the late 1990s, it did not carry the day. By 2005, the German government passed a law aimed at extending the provision of child care for all children under three years old. Christian Leipert and Michael Opielka, *Child-Care Salary 2000: A Way to Up-Grade Child Care Work* (Institute for Social Ecology: Bonn, Ger., 1999).

31. For a detailed analysis of the three dominant European child-care models, see Rianne Mahon, "Child Care: Toward What Kind of 'Social Europe'?" *Social Politics*, Fall 2002, 343–379.

32. Norwegian Ministry of Children and Family Affairs, "Day Care Policy in Norway," http://www.norway.org/policy/family/daycare/daycare.htm.

33. The home-care allowances were cut back substantially in 1995 accompanied by a 3 percent decline in the Finnish birthrate the next year. Jorma Sipila and Johanna Korpinin, "Cash versus Child Care Services in Finland," *Social Policy and Administration* 32, no. 3 (September 1998), 263–277.

34. In recent times, however, there have been some reports of companies trying to build better "on-ramps" for women wishing to return to work after a time-out for childrearing. See McGinn, "Getting Back on Track."

35. French Embassy, "Family Policy in France," http://www.ambafrance-us.org/atoz/fam_pol.asp.

36. Department of Further Education Employment and Technology, *Program Guidelines for Parents* (Adelaide: Government of South Australia, 2005).

37. More than twenty years ago, in an earlier version of this social credit proposal, I considered providing credits for each year spent at home with children under seventeen years of age. Since then I've lowered the age, having gone through the teenage years with two of my children. See Neil Gilbert, "In Support of Domesticity."

38. Nicholas Barr and Fiona Coulter, "Social Security: Solution or Problem?" in John Hills, ed., *The State of Welfare: The Welfare State in Britain since 1974* (Oxford: Oxford University Press, 1990); Martin Tracy and Patsy Tracy, "The Treatment of Women as Dependents under Social Security: After 50 Years How Does the United States Compare with Other Countries?" *Journal of Applied Social Sciences* 11, no. 1 (1987), 5–16.

39. For a review of these schemes, see Hans-Joachim Reinhard, "The Splitting of Pension Credits in the Federal Republic of Germany and Canada—An Appropriate Way to Achieve Equality in Social Security Treatment for Men and Women?" in *Equal Treatment in Social Security,* Studies and Research no. 27 (Geneva: International Social Security Association, 1988).

40. OECD, *Shaping Structural Change: The Role of Women* (Paris: OECD, 1991).

41. Hedwige Peemans-Poullet, "The Individualization of Rights," paper presented at the European Regional Meeting of the International Social Security Association, Luxembourg, May 19–21, 1999, p. 72.

42. Substituting a credit-sharing scheme for the dependents' allowance would lead to a reduction in benefits for the traditional one-earner family and divorced men, which was seen as a serious problem. By the late 1980s credit-sharing reforms were off the political agenda. However, a proposal to split social security entitlements resurfaced under Title IV of the Economic Equity Act introduced in Congress in 1992. Current prospects for this type of reform remain faint. For the background see Jane Ross and Melinda Upp, "The Treatment of Women in the United States Social Security System," in *Equal Treatment in Social Security,* Studies and research no. 27 (Geneva: International Social Security Association, 1988).

43. Ann Crittenden, *The Price of Motherhood* (New York: Henry Holt), 12.

Index